MW01034639

WHEN EVENING COMES

WHEN EVENING COMES

COMES

The Education of a Hospice Volunteer

Christine Andreae

THOMAS DUNNE BOOKS
St. Martin's Press
New York

THOMAS DUNNE BOOKS.
An imprint of St. Martin's Press.

www.stmartins.com

Poem on p. ix. "Let Evening Come" copyright 1996 by the estate of Jane
Kenyon. Reprinted from *Otherwise: New & Selected Poems* with the
permission of Graywolf Press, Saint Paul, Minnesota.

Lines on p. 126 from "Burnt Norton" from *Four Quartets* by T. S. Eliot.
Copyright 1936 by Harcourt, Inc. and renewed 1964 by T. S. Eliot, reprinted by permission of the publisher.

Lines on p. 138 from *Fruit Gathering* by Rabindranath Tagore (New York:
Macmillan, 1916) reprinted with permission.

Lines on p. 143 from "Landscape With Tractor" by Henry Taylor copyright
1986 by Henry Taylor. Reprinted from *The Flying Change* by permission of
the author and LSU Press.

Book design by Tim Hall

Library of Congress Cataloging-in-Publication Data

Andreae, Christine.
    When evening comes : the education of a hospice volunteer / Christine
Andreae.
        p. cm.
    ISBN 0-312-26871-8
    1. Hospice care. 2. Volunteer workers in community health services—
Diaries. 3. Volunteer workers in hospitals—Diaries. I. Title.
R726.8 .A54   2000
362.1'756—dc21
                                                            00-040249

First Edition: October 2000

10   9   8   7   6   5   4   3   2   1

To my husband, Andy,
who was always there, even when I wasn't

AUTHOR'S NOTE

IN writing down these end-of-life stories, I have tried to be a true witness to events as they unfolded. The experiences described are not exceptional; the only "exceptional" aspect of these stories is the fact that I happen to have written them down. For me, writing things down is part of my private learning curve. But there are thousands of hospice workers all over the country and each one has unwritten stories that are at once amazing and commonplace, stories in which the unique and the universal converge.

"Bivie," the first section of this book, was privately published in 1995 as *One Woman's Death* by Blue Ridge Hospice. It is published here with the permission of Blue Ridge Hospice and the Peterson family. Then as now, it is with affection and love that I acknowledge the unfailing support of Greg Peterson and his parents, Dorothy and Keith Peterson, who reviewed the manuscript for factual errors. In "Amber," the second section, I have changed names and identifying details. Where I have used real names, it is with permission. I am especially grateful to Frances Charles, who graciously read and corrected my account of her mother's last months.

I am indebted to the Blue Ridge Hospice staff, board members, and volunteers, past and present, who have given me support and shared their insights. Special thanks to Chris and Lisa Curran, who served as editors and publishers of *One Woman's Death*, to Nate Adams, Lynne Sayles, and Helen Zebarth, a

founding mother of our hospice; to Nikki Hill, Caroline Hast-
reiter, and Rhonda Headley; to Ernie Carnevale, Mare Rockwood,
Marian Gaynor, Charlotte Stanton, Pam Wisor, Brigit Blevins,
Peg Jackson, Phyllis Maloy, and Cinnamon Huie.

It is literally true to say that without Anne Holliday, this
book never would have been written. The deaths of Anne's
daughter, Hosanna, and her husband, Mark, led me to hospice,
and her openness and courage have always been an inspiration
for me. I also want to thank my friends who, over the years, have
encouraged me to write about my hospice patients: Theresa
Curry, Suzanne Kilgore, Anna Collins. Thanks to Harry Papagan,
whose generous heart and critical eye helped shape this manuscript. Finally, thanks to Jane Chelius, my agent, and to Ruth
Cavin, my editor, both of whom believed that real-life stories
about dying need to be told.

Let Evening Come

by Jane Kenyon

Let the light of late afternoon
shine through chinks in the barn, moving
up the bales as the sun moves down.

Let the cricket take up chafing
as a woman takes up her needles
and her yarn. Let evening come.

Let dew collect on the hoe abandoned
in long grass. Let the stars appear
and the moon disclose her silver horn.

Let the fox go back to its sandy den.
Let the wind die down. Let the shed
go black inside. Let evening come.

To the bottle in the ditch, to the scoop
in the oats, to air in the lung
let evening come.

Let it come, as it will, and don't
be afraid. God does not leave us
comfortless, so let evening come.

1991

BIVIE

I do not know whether I was then
a man dreaming I was a butterfly,
or whether I am now a butterfly dreaming
I am a man.

—Chuang-tzu (369–286 B.C.)

A month after Bivie Peterson, my first hospice patient, died, I talked on the phone with her husband, Greg—a big, soft-spoken man who was not comfortable discussing the interior landscape of his grief. I asked him, "How's it going?" He reflected a moment, then said, "Okay, I guess." End of answer.

So we talked about black-footed ferrets. These are rare, weasel-like creatures who once inhabited the prairies of the American West, and are now on the edge of extinction. Greg is a zookeeper in charge of the black-footed ferrets at the National Zoo's Conservation and Research Center outside the town of Front Royal in Virginia's Shenandoah Valley. During Bivie's last days, the conservation center's female ferrets came into estrus. Greg helped keep a round-the-clock mating vigil. There was nothing he could do to rescue Bivie from her death, but perhaps there was some small comfort in knowing he was helping to rescue a species from extinction. A month later, the female ferrets were about to give birth. He sounded pleased and excited by the prospect. It was as if in some obscure masculine way, he was telling me that "life goes on"—that he was healing. Bivie, I think, would have approved. Perhaps she would have even sighed with relief: *Well, it's okay then.* She was a caregiver, a manager.

In 1988, I joined the board of Blue Ridge Hospice as a grantwriter. I liked writing grants. I liked the money. It pleased me to know I had earned more money for hospice than I ever earned as a freelance writer. It made me feel fiscally real, something more than a housewife who scribbles on the side.

I also liked the pure technical puzzle of grantwriting. I found it challenging to decipher the logic of donors' rules and I enjoyed shaping a complicated request that was lucid and tightly constructed. In a well-crafted grant application, the various parts—the narrative, the financials, the supporting documents—are as interdependent as the pieces of a wooden puzzle cube. Writing a grant proposal is a rational exercise. When and if the money comes in, one can bask in the illusion that reason has triumphed. Twenty-five thousand dollars in grant money makes it easy to believe that the universe is an ordered place where clear thinking and clear writing are justly rewarded.

I am still not very clear about what prompted me to sign up for twenty-seven hours of patient-care training. At the time, I told myself that the training would help me write better grants. Perhaps it did. Be that as it may, in October of 1990, I took the course. There were about forty of us, mostly women, mostly middle-aged or older. For four days from nine to four, we watched films on death and dying and blew our noses into Kleenex. We sucked on hard candy and listened to oncologists and undertakers, a psychologist, a hospital chaplain, and a hospice nurse talk about cancer, pain control, funeral costs, family dynamics, bereavement, the spiritual needs of dying people, their physical needs. The question-and-answer sessions were lively. Most of our questions started out the same: "What I am supposed to do if . . . ?" "How do I deal with . . . ?"

We ate brown-bag lunches and talked matter-of-factly about our own encounters with death. I was surprised how many at my table had suffered acute losses: husbands, children, parents. My own parents, my husband, Andy, and our two sons were all alive and well.

Two things happened at the training that deeply impressed

me. The first was an impromptu lesson on what is entailed in being nonjudgmental. A funeral director was taking questions. A woman raised her hand and said, "I knew some people whose baby died and they wanted to have a viewing." She hesitated.

"Yes?" encouraged the funeral director.

"Well, they wanted to have their baby sitting up in her playpen with all her toys around?"

There was a communal gasp of horror.

But before the undertaker could open his mouth to assure her that, yes, this kind of arrangement could be made, Caroline Hastreiter, our trainer and then the Director of Blue Ridge Hospice, jumped to her feet.

"Excuse me," she said to the funeral director. He yielded the podium to her. "I am so glad this happened," she said to us. The earnestness in her voice squelched our giggles. "Because if *your* patient's family expresses a similar wish, you *cannot* gasp. Your jaw *cannot* drop open. You *cannot* let them know *in any way* that you think the idea is disgusting. You are there to help them, *not* to impose your own tastes and preferences on them."

My second unforgettable "learning experience" was a nasty little game. Caroline called it a "sensitivity exercise." She asked us to take a blank piece of paper and a pencil and list the six most important things in our lives. We groaned and wisecracked. "They can be people, places, things," she instructed. "Whatever you value most in your life."

We groaned some more. But the assignment was intriguing.

"Can I put my family down as one thing or do I have to list them separately?" someone asked.

Caroline smiled. "However you like."

I raised my hand. "Are we going to have to show each other these lists?" I asked.

"No," Caroline answered. She gave us five minutes, then instructed, "Okay. Now cross off three things on your list."

We complained. "I'll tell you one thing," said a woman at the next table, "I'll give up my husband before I give up my dog." She sounded serious.

"Ready?" Caroline asked. "Now cross off two more things on your list."

The group mood became sober. I thought to myself: *I get it. She's trying to get us to examine our priorities.* I crossed off two more things. I clearly remember a small sinking feeling: I was crossing off the wrong things; my premises for my choices were wrong.

"Okay," Caroline announced. "Now cross off the last thing." We stared at her.

"Everyone who is dying goes through this process," she explained. "Eventually, they have to let go of everything precious in their lives. You found the exercise hard. Some of you even felt angry. Imagine if it were for real."

My first contact with death was seeing our aged parish priest laid out in his coffin. My father had taken my sister and me to "pay our respects." Perhaps I was five or six. The priest looked small and waxy in a black cassock with little buttons down the front. The coffin, however, was a puzzle. It stood high over my head on a black-skirted bier. Why was it blocking the church's center aisle? And why was the priest lying on *top* of a blanket of white flowers? My father said, "What flowers?" (I think now what I saw must have been puffs of quilted white satin lining.) I also remember my mother's tacit distaste when we got home and my father told her where we had been. On my mother's side of the family, a body—once the person who inhabited it was gone—was a private thing, not to be displayed and gaped at. Growing up, I attended the funeral masses of my maternal grandparents and great aunts, but there were no "viewings." In fact, for me, all the deaths in my family occurred "offstage," in a hospital.

The first time I became involved with the actual process of dying was in rural Virginia in 1975. My husband and I and our two sons, then ages four years and six months, had moved from Washington, D.C., to the Shenandoah Valley to build a house in the woods. As it happened, a countercultural community had taken over an abandoned Boy Scout camp across the road. We became friends with Anne Holliday, an English midwife and RN, and her husband Mark Holliday, a chiropractor from South Carolina. They lived in a geodesic dome with their five children. When their youngest daughter Hosanna was four—the same age as our oldest son—Mark discovered a tumor on her spine. She was hospitalized at the University of Virginia's Medical Center in Charlottesville. There, after weeks of testing, oncologists pronounced the cancer "inoperable." Mark and Anne brought Hosanna home from the hospital. At first I was shocked that they had done this: surely the place for a child that sick was in the hospital and not in a leaky, galvanized tin dome out in the middle of the woods. Later I marveled at the care they gave her. Only parents with medical training could manage it, I thought.

My involvement was the neighborly sort. I helped out with food, took the older children to play with my own. I had little direct contact with Hosanna, though on occasion, after a bad night, Anne would load her into the back of my VW wagon and we would drive the back roads while Hosanna, soothed by the motion of the car, would finally doze off. After a long, muggy summer, she died on the second of November, the Feast of All Souls. The women in the community helped Anne wash Hosanna's body. The men made a plywood box. The walnut stain wasn't quite dry when they lowered it on ropes into a hillside grave. Everyone sang "He's Got the Whole World in His Hands" and took a turn with the shovels. Children scrambled over the slowly diminishing pile of red clay and threw dried-out stalks of Queen Anne's lace down into the hole.

Later that year, I went along with Anne to a home birthing in a trailer. Like Hosanna's death, the births Anne attended as a state-approved "granny woman" were communal events. Friends crowded around the mother's bed and cheered and hugged each other and wept with joy and relief. When I had pushed out my own babies, I'd been surrounded by strangers in green masks. I was not about to give up hospitals and their life-saving technologies. But in the trailer's crush of supportive friends, it suddenly seemed peculiar that for most of us, birth and death occur in isolation. Why, I wondered, has our culture removed our family and friends from the two most critical processes in our lives, being born and dying?

I still wonder about this. Certainly one of the reasons I am drawn to hospice is that it brings the process of dying back into the community. "Home death" is not a hospice goal. Our mission is to provide support to the dying and their families—wherever the death occurs. But if asked to envision the ideal circumstances for a death, most hospice workers would imagine the patient in his or her own bed, surrounded by family and friends. It is a scene more common to Victorian literature than to our time.

I first learned about hospice as a reporter. At the time, I was freelancing for *Virginia Country*. The magazine's publisher and editor, the late Garrison Ellis, who had been called both "perverse" and "courageous" for tackling the taboo, had already printed a number of difficult articles I'd written—explorations of incest and child sexual abuse, of domestic violence, of a local murder. In 1985, Garry and I talked about doing a piece on death and dying. I contacted Blue Ridge Hospice and talked at length with staff and patient-care volunteers—all of whom, at that time, were women. Garry subtitled the article "Midwives to Death" and ran it along with recipes for Christmas cookies in the December issue. This time, there were no complaints from subscribers—somewhat to Garry's disappointment, I suspect.

During the research for this article, I began to more fully appreciate Anne and Mark's decision to bring Hosanna home. They had faced her death in a way that I had not. They had let go of hope of a cure—as much as any parent can. I know Mark kept hoping for the miracle of spontaneous remission. And since they had not devoted all their energies to denying her illness, they had been able to focus on "the quality of remaining life"—to use a hospice cliché. It seemed an extraordinarily brave and sensible parental stance.

But if I was in awe of the way Mark and Anne had managed their daughter's death, I had to wonder about the hospice volunteers. They were not taking care of their own. They were going into the houses of strangers. Why? They looked like nice, ordinary women. They wore makeup and pretty sweaters and stockings. "Isn't it stressful?" I asked one volunteer.

"There's no real stress," she answered serenely. "It's caring and sharing, and feeling and loving. That's not frustrating."

"It's very consuming," explained another, more down-to-earth volunteer. "But once you've dealt with your own fear of death, it's not stressful."

They spoke of "giving," of "unconditional love," then objected, "It sounds so sappy!" They discussed the strange way in which their patients seemed to choose their own moment of death. They talked about the experience of "something going on" in the moments after a death. Even the most skeptical of them wondered at the mystery of it. Sometimes their eyes shone with tears. More often they laughed. I admired them. I admired their commitment. But most of all, I admired their nerve. Here was a group of women who cheerfully declared that they were not afraid of death. Here was a group of women who ventured into territory the rest of us preferred to avoid.

The following year, Mark Holliday complained of a pain in his shoulder. It proved to be cancer—in the advanced stages. By this time, our countercultural neighbors had dispersed and Mark and Anne were living in a small town further down the Valley. The family had little money. Although Mark was licensed to practice as a chiropractor in South Carolina, after his daughter's death, he seemed to lose interest in obtaining a Virginia license. He worked at a series of jobs while Anne taught nursing. When Mark became sick, Anne could not afford to stop teaching and stay home with him. At the same time, she did not want to leave him alone in the house all day. Friends set up a rotating "sitting" schedule. I took three afternoons a week.

The idea of sitting with a dying friend was a great deal worse than the reality—at least at the outset. I had not spent a lot of time with Mark; it was Anne and I who had forged a bond through our children. So there was the pleasure of getting to know this man—this husband of my friend who seemed to grow more handsome as his illness ate away middle-aged pounds and his morphine smoothed away stress lines. We treated each other with formal courtesy. We had no deep discussions. He told me he didn't want to "get philosophical" about his dying. Sometimes I would read while he dozed in the next room and the way the autumn sun slanted across my paperback seemed impossibly luxurious. Sometimes I drove him on errands: to an orchard to buy apples for his youngest son's school lunch; to the supermarket where a bunch of broccoli he picked up suddenly became incandescent. I used to look forward to those afternoons. I dressed with care and brought him the last bunches of marigolds and zinnias that grew in our vegetable garden. All this earned me a rather embarrassing—if secretly satisfying—halo.

As Mark's condition deteriorated, Anne called in hospice.

Mark's volunteer was Nikki Hill, a nurse who later joined the hospice staff. The older children came home from college to help with the demands of round-the-clock care. The family took turns sleeping on a mattress on the floor beside his bed. Despite the morphine, Mark suffered a lot of pain. Waltzing in and out with my halo didn't help anymore. I learned things about myself I didn't like. But I also learned that strength and courage are infectious—we can, in fact, "catch" them from each other. And when Mark finally "checked out" (as he wryly used to put it), I learned that a "good" death cannot be measured only in terms of swiftness and ease: a "good" death has to do with love—and with that tidying-up process called forgiveness.

On the last day of my patient-care training, just before we all went home, we played yet another game. We arranged our chairs in a large circle and Caroline passed around a tray filled with various small objects: feathers, plastic pearls and rubies, a book of matches, a paper daisy, a flashlight bulb, a length of string, a curtain ring, a rubber band, a pebble, a piece of driftwood, a button—the kind of junk that tends to accumulate in kitchen drawers. She asked each of us to pick an object that represented what we felt we had to give to someone who was dying.

We went around the circle explaining our choices. People spoke movingly and at some length. The statement "I'm a warm, caring person" kept coming up. As my turn came closer, I felt panicky. It had never occurred to me to define myself as a "warm, caring person." Was I supposed to characterize myself? Was this part of the assignment? What came to mind was: "I'm a curious person." But this smacked of voyeurism.

To make matters worse, I really had no idea why I had chosen what I did. I had been aware that it was taking me a long time to pick an object, maybe too long. Finally, I snatched up a key and passed the tray to my neighbor. The key was brass with elaborate designs impressed into its top. It had an old-fashioned look and felt cool and heavy in the hand. I closed my fingers around it and found its hardness reassuring. When it was my turn to speak, I invented something about "wanting to help open doors for people." I flushed as if I were lying. Looking back, it occurs to me that perhaps I was. Perhaps what I wanted was to open a door for myself.

Nikki Hill (hospice nurse and patient-care coordinator) has assigned me a patient. I took the training to learn more about hospice; I had no intention of taking on a patient. But flattery works. Both Caroline and Nikki told me that this was a special case and that I'd be "perfect" for it.

This is what Nikki told me on the phone: Bivie Peterson is thirty-nine years old. In October, while I was taking patient-care training, Bivie discovered she had cancer of the colon. In November, she had a colostomy.

"During the surgery, they found 'mets' on her liver," Nikki said, her voice grim. "She knows what that means."

Greg Peterson, her husband, works at the Conservation Center and has three daughters from a previous marriage. The two oldest are away at boarding school. Monica, who is thirteen, is at home. Greg and Bivie have been married five years and have two children, both girls. A five-year-old and a twenty-month-old baby. "Bivie probably had the cancer when she was pregnant with the baby," Nikki guesses. "Now she's on chemo."

The family moved out here from Alexandria just before she was diagnosed. She doesn't know anyone. Her father died of colon cancer a year ago. Her mother died a couple years before that. Nikki says she's still grieving for her father.

How do you deal with your own death while mourning someone else's? How do you deal with your own death while taking care of your baby?

"She's not a typical cancer patient," Nikki tells me. "She doesn't *look* like she has cancer. She might have more than six months." Nikki's voice brightens at the prospect. "She's a *neat* lady!" Nikki exclaims. "You'll really like her!" The idea of "fixing me up" with her patient excites her. Nikki the Matchmaker. I can't help smiling.

JANUARY 25, FRIDAY

Called Bivie and introduced myself. This was not easy. "Hi, I want to help you die," is the message, even if the actual words are somewhat more circumspect. But she talked frankly about her disease. She said she thought hospice was wonderful. She said she hoped to be able to "give something back to it." The winter sun was streaming through my windows. I gushed, "Oh, but you will!" She sounded disconcerted. I tried to explain and couldn't. The words had just popped out of my mouth. I felt embarrassed. My enthusiasm seemed impolite.

She asked me what I did and I told her I was a writer. I also told her I was teaching composition at our community college. She said she'd always wanted to write a book. She wanted to leave something for her daughters, to set down memories that otherwise would be lost.

We agreed to meet for coffee at the Palace Cafe on Main Street in Front Royal. Neutral turf. Maybe she wasn't ready to let me in her house. On the other hand, maybe she wanted time off from her kids. Maybe it allowed her to say to her husband, "I need to meet this woman from hospice. Will you baby-sit for a couple hours?" We decided on Friday, at two in the afternoon. She had her chemo on Mondays and usually felt better on Fridays.

I attempted to describe myself so she would recognize me. I

said I was tall with dark brown hair going gray. Then I got stuck. I told her I'd be wearing a lavender blue parka.

She sounded pleased. She said her hair was also dark brown going gray. She said she still had it all, despite the chemo. She hadn't even lost weight. She laughed. "I'm a chubbette," she said. She was disappointed that chemo hadn't made her svelte. "I guess my weight will come in handy later on," she consoled herself. Before we hung up she said it again: "I'm a chubbette."

FEBRUARY 1, FRIDAY

She walked into the Palace Cafe, five minutes late. I had taken off my parka and draped it like a lavender flag over the back of the booth. We recognized each other immediately.

I don't know what I expected her to look like. Maybe I thought she'd have a beauty shop hairdo. But it was thick, straight, shoulder-length, blacker than brown, shot with single white hairs, and swinging with health and vitality. Not your typical cancer patient, Nikki had warned. She had a hundred-and-twenty-watt, movie-star smile. Her eyes were observant, her face pretty. "Chubbette" is the wrong word. (I should have told her.) It suggests a cheerleader gone to fat. Bivie is a big woman, but her aura, her energy isn't fat and wobbly. She wore a lavender jersey tunic, loose enough to hide her colostomy bag. The tunic was almost the same shade as my parka.

"Oh," she said. "You are a beautiful woman!"

Of course I loved her immediately. I couldn't think when anyone had said that to me. Had Andy never told me? Have I forgotten? I remember my grandmother used to praise my eyes. "Shoe-button eyes," she would say humorously—a reference to Raggedy Ann.

Bivie and I traded oral resumes of our lives. I gave her *Writing Down the Bones*, Natalie Goldberg's encouragements on keeping a journal. Mostly she talked about the needs of her family, her baby, her five-year-old, her three teenage stepdaughters who were all over two hundred pounds, and were coming to stay for the summer. She complained that they lie around the house and never lift a finger. I thought of my long skinny teenage sons who lie in bed all morning, then can't find the energy to flip their dirty underwear into a laundry bin.

Her conflicts with her stepdaughters worried her. She was concerned about "being positive"—as if anger could rev up her cancer.

"Do you get time to look out the window?" I asked.

"I try to do that in between."

We smiled. I remembered what it was like having a two-year-old.

Suddenly it was time for her to go. I had finished my salad and was on my third cup of decaf. She had made valiant stabs at her salad, but mostly drank ice water in a tall, pebbled plastic glass. I worried that I hadn't been "working." Hurriedly I said, "I feel as if you've been talking mostly about the needs of other people. Are you considering your own needs?"

Her reaction was neutral, polite.

Now I'm thinking: Not swift. *You just stuck another burden on her. You just told her she should be thinking more of herself.*

Out on the sidewalk I meet Greg, her husband, her five-year-old, and her thirteen-year-old stepdaughter. They had all come to pick her up. Greg is a big man with a graying brown beard and a kindness about him. Sara, the five-year-old, is snappy and bright and skinny. Monica, the thirteen-year-old, is big and blonde and pink. She clung to her father, burying her face in his sleeve like a much younger child. We looked each other over. They seemed concerned, willing, uncertain.

FEBRUARY 6, WEDNESDAY

On Monday the oncologist refused Bivie her chemo treatment. The level of toxicity in her body was too high. This morning on the phone, Bivie sounded relieved, cheerful even. Her interpretation: If I don't have to have it, I'm doing better.

Nikki's interpretation: Bad news. It's not working.

Caroline Hastreiter (hospice director), wants me to get Bivie's "story" for the hospice. Bivie is enthusiastic. She says she started reading *Writing Down the Bones*, but despaired of finding the time and energy to sit down and actually *write*. I tell her not to worry, I can get her on tape. We talk about putting together a kind of double diary, hers and mine. We are both excited by this.

She keeps saying she wants to be "positive." She has been thinking about which pieces of her jewelry she wants to leave to which daughter. But instead of getting pleasure from the decisions, instead of imagining them grown and beautiful in her pearls and turquoise and antique carnelian, she worries about being "negative." She worries that negative thoughts will encourage her disease.

I feel like burning all those "self-heal" books that suggest cures are possible if patients will only "accept responsibility" for their disease.

I tell her I think she is being practical. I tell her that I don't believe thinking about one's death is necessarily negative. I tell her that getting those kinds of decisions out of the way might give her a sense of freedom. I tell her she is one of the most positive people I've ever met.

"Oh, that's good to hear," she says. Then she apologizes. "I guess, being the oldest child in my family, I need a lot of reinforcement."

"I'm the oldest too," I say.

We talk about fat. We talk about how much we weighed

when. We are more worried about fat than death. A hundred years ago Bivie's size would have been considered part of her beauty. A hundred years ago thin was unhealthy. Orphans and beggars and consumptives were skinny. The rich bloomed flesh. John Singer Sargent painted them looking pleased about it.

Bivie says the tumor cut out of her bowel was seven inches long. She says she ignored the bleeding. She thought she had hemorrhoids. Who has been pregnant and *not* had hemorrhoids?

FEBRUARY 15, FRIDAY

Olivia, Bivie's almost-two-year-old is sick. Bivie is reluctant to take her to the clinic in town. It's not only a matter of the long wait to get into the doctor, but fear of catching something from the children in the waiting room. She says the chemo makes her vulnerable to infection. So I call our pediatrician and explain the situation. She gives Livia an afternoon appointment and says that Bivie can wait in a private room. Bivie seems relieved. At the clinic the girls never saw the same doctor twice in a row. She says she's been looking for "continuity in care" for the girls.

FEBRUARY 16, SATURDAY MORNING

We talk on the phone. She does not want me to visit. Greg has taken the children into D.C. She wants to keep the day for herself. She wants to make sense of her medical bills. It is impossible to spread out the paperwork when Olivia is around. "Livia is a regular pistol!" she says proudly. But she sounds bone-tired.

She says she has always managed the family finances and now she is going to have to teach Greg how to manage. "He's real vague about his checkbook."

She has a headache and blames it on the medication she is taking for a bladder infection. She has been miserable all week with it. She kept thinking the cancer was getting bigger and putting pressure on her insides, so she was relieved when the doctor told her it was a bladder infection.

She worries about the end. "I can deal with pain," she tells me. "I'm pretty good at handling it. I just wonder if I'll be able to manage it at the end."

I tell her what the oncologists (one of whom is hers) said at my training: that rarely does a person dying of cancer have to deal with massive pain. "But you might have to choose between being knocked out and being in pain," I warn her. "Some people find it frustrating to feel so drugged." I was thinking of my friend Mark who died of cancer five years before.

Bivie also worries about being cross with her children. "I snap at them too often," she frets. She doesn't want them to remember her as a royal bitch. But she feels rotten more than half the time. She has morning battles over clothes with Sara, the five-year-old. Sara tells her angrily, "You're going away. I hate you. I'm going to get a new mother."

Bivie *is* going away in March. She and Greg are going on a week-long Caribbean cruise. The trip is a gift from his parents. She plans to stop chemo the week before so she'll feel better.

Again, she tells me she wants to write a book. She is an Ayn Rand fan. "I'd like to write about the grandeur of man," she says wistfully.

FEBRUARY 26, TUESDAY

Bivie was supposed to have had more chemo on Monday, but again they withheld it. Nikki called me about it. "I hope she gets to go on her cruise," she worried. "Get in there and do the tapes for her daughters," she said.

This sets me back. I'd counted on her having more time to live. Meeting her was such a high. And the idea of a keeping a double journal has been exhilarating.

I keep thinking of the way one of the volunteers I interviewed for *Virginia Country* described hospice work: what she liked about it was the way it "cut away all the crap" that we put up with in ordinary relationships. "When someone's dying," she said, "you can get right to the point."

I wanted to get to the point with Bivie—to love, or acceptance, or whatever the point is. I imagined going on this kind of pure, intense trip with her. Two weeks ago, it seemed possible. I was soaring along on love for her. But now I'm wading in crap: my own fears and insecurities, plus the physical business of her death.

This morning, I talk to Bivie on the phone. She is frustrated by not knowing what is going on in her body. First she thought it was all just a bladder infection. Now she's not sure. Her periods have gone haywire (chemo effect, Nikki says). She has sprouted black hairs on her chin, and a little white patch of down on the very tip of her nose. "What does that mean?" she asks me.

Neither of us had ever heard of such a thing. She and Greg joke about it. "My bunny nose," she calls it.

Of her failed chemotherapy, she says, "There's only a thirty-five percent positive result. So statistically, it's not surprising that it hasn't worked for me." She's ready to try something else.

I don't want her to shut me out. How can I tell her this without sounding like a ghoul?

"I'm not planning on dying soon," she tells me. It is almost a rebuke. Does she *know* that she has the time she wants? Or is it denial at work? She is a manager, a person who flourishes making arrangements. She prides herself on staying on top of things, on being in control. She was in the food-service business: she *fed* people.

She tells me she went to look for a new bathing suit for her cruise and met a woman in the dressing rooms who said that she, too, was a cancer patient—bowel cancer that had gotten into the liver—and that had been five years ago. "I needed to meet you today!" Bivie told her.

Bivie tells me the story and laughs. It takes my breath away. To both of us the woman in the dressing room seems miraculous, a sign. Hope wings back and forth between our phones.

But can hope stop the spread of her cancer? Nikki is skeptical about the story of remission. "Maybe I'm being too pessimistic," she says. "All my patients die." She can count only two who were discharged from the program. In neither case had the cancer gone to the liver.

I find myself wanting to peer inside my own body. Everything okay in there, guys? Liver? Should I stop drinking so much white wine? Lungs? Did I stop smoking in time? What's that twinge, this bump?

At the same time, I don't want to know anything. I just want my body to politely keep on going, like my car, squarish, comfortable. Forget about speed and chic.

Of course I don't. In the Nautilus room, I add more weight to the machines and pump away to the radio's selection of mediocre old rock.

If I were going to die next year, I'd order icy martinis in stemmed glasses with five gin-soaked olives. I'd cook with butter again and pig out on brie and triple crème. I'd throw away herb teas and drink black French Roast coffee and old red wine. I'd start Marlboros again. I'd smoke away my fat and get lean as a twenty-five-year-old and lie out in the sun and get as brown as a gypsy.

Is that what I'd do? Or would I keep trying to stay pure, driven by the hope of adding extra time onto my year?

Bivie says the pain is like a sharp stitch in her side, the kind you get from running, but it's constant. The doctor has given her Percocet, which worked at first, but now seems not to. It makes her feel sleepy, dopey. When she picked up the phone her voice was very far away and weak. She was lying on the couch with Livia watching *Sesame Street*.

Livia interrupts most of our phone conversations. The TV does not hold her. She climbs on chairs, tries to change channels, falls, cries. This time, Bivie coaxes her into getting her own bottle. "She's beginning to be able to follow instructions," Bivie says wearily. The effort to get off the couch and get the wretched bottle is too much for her.

"Can you read at all?" I ask her.

"With an almost two-year-old?" she demands. Her voice is humorous, but I feel the frustration.

"I forgot," I apologize.

"Your kids are grown. I can't imagine it." She laughs.

The unspoken question nudges us: will she see her daughters grown?

I tell her we'll make some tapes for her girls. I tell her I hope she'll be there to give them to them when they graduate from high school. There's a silence. I tell her I'm thinking of her all the time. She thanks me. We hang up.

MARCH 1, FRIDAY

Nikki called around noon. Bivie was over at the Cancer Center in the morning to get the results of Tuesday's CAT scan from her doctor. The news is not good. Her cancer has become aggressive. It is growing in her liver, and there are nodes in her neck. The "girls in chemo" (as Nikki calls them) were upset. They hugged Bivie and she broke down. "She kept apologizing for it," Nikki said.

Nikki had hugged her too. "I needed to," she says. "I thought maybe I picked up some signals that she didn't want me to hug her, but I needed to do it for me, so I did." She wonders if it was a mistake. "She may not want me near her. It may be just a personality thing. She may do better with you." Nikki sounds disappointed. I tell her I feel held at bay too. I tell her that Bivie and I have good phone conversations but she doesn't seem to want me in her house.

"How long do you think she has?" I ask.

"Maybe a couple of months," Nikki estimates. Then quickly she adds, "But there's always surprises, reversals."

The doctor told her to go ahead on her cruise, but warned her that she might not feel well on it. She went to the appointment with her purse stuffed full of bills and she worked on them in the waiting room. She appears determined to stay in control of her household, but finds it harder and harder on account of the pain. The doctor gave her some morphine capsules. She popped them down and drove herself home. She refused to let Nikki drive her. Nikki worried about her getting home safely. "At least they're time-release capsules," she tried to reassure herself.

We agreed that I should wait a couple of days before calling Bivie. This will give her a chance to adjust to the doctor's bad news.

———————

I work out. Afterward, hunched over in the sauna, I feel drops of sweat trickle down my back, down behind my ears, down the sides of my breasts. It drips off my nose like fat tears. A detached, painless sort of crying.

Meanwhile, my mind buzzes obsessively. I drive home, peel garlic, fold clothes out of the dryer, pour a glass of wine, and all the time I'm making up conversations in my head with her: How to tell her I think she is beautiful; how to tell her I think I can help; all without having her slam the door in my face.

MARCH 3, SUNDAY

Called Bivie around 4:30 P.M. Rainy dark afternoon. My daffodils are blooming in fistfuls in the south-exposed woods.

She was cooking dinner with Greg's help. She told me her news. She said the morphine worked—it took the pain away, but not the discomfort. "I feel as if I have too many organs inside me," she joked.

We were rather businesslike. She doesn't want too much sympathy, but likes encouragement and praise. So I told her I thought she was great, that she was handling everything so well. "I'm a controller," she burst out sarcastically. She was cooking dinner and talking to me about her cancer at the same time.

She doesn't feel that handling it "badly" is a choice. "What else is there to do?" she demands.

"Lie down and cry about it."

She laughs. "I did some of that too."

"Don't you think it would be peculiar if you didn't?"

"Well . . ." A begrudging allowance on the other end of the line.

She wants to see me. She says it a couple times.

She tells me that her oncologist wants to have a catheter inserted into a vein in her neck so he can give her a round-the-clock chemo drip. She wants to question him about this, to ask what the odds are, what the alternatives are. She wonders about steroids, maybe, to shrink swelling and make her more comfortable. She is in a managerial mode about her cancer, her prescriptions. She jokes about wanting some speed. "Why not?" I ask. I'm not joking.

We talk about finding a temporary bookkeeper for her.

We talk about our "journal." I tell her that I'll bring my tape recorder, that I've been thinking about how to go about making a tape for her daughters. I say I want her to think about what it was like when she was carrying them, what they were like as babies, how she and Greg met and married. "Every child wants to know how their parents got together," I say.

"I was three months pregnant when we got married!" she announces.

We laugh. Good material, we agree.

If we can get the tape for the girls out of the way, then I'll think about a hospice-type interview—something for other patients?

I am easier now about being accepted. To keep it going I need to work with her style. Stiff-upper lip shouldn't be all that hard for me. Even if mine isn't, I've lived with enough of them to fake it.

Or call it being professional. Bivie and I can be a pair of professional women dealing with her death.

Her death.

The volunteer training was supposed to help me accept my own, to lose fear by becoming familiar with the fact of it. I had this misty notion that one day I'd be there, serenely accepting of my death and therefore able to help other people do the same. Now I'm thinking this is a crock. How can we ever really accept the *reality* of it? Each of us has a survival drive programmed in the core of each gene. At that particular moment in time when we really and truly embrace our own death—then we're gone.

The pain of death is the peeling away. I have this image of a thick-skinned fruit. Bivie, in her dying, first pares away neatly scored slices of rind, then one by one, the internal segments. The managerial aspect is choosing which piece goes first, which next?

Then you're down to nothing. What's next in that emptiness? What happens to that center around which there was once, say, an orange?

Does it matter? This unknown *Next*? I'm thinking the way to stay on track here is to hold on tight to the *Now*.

MARCH 6, WEDNESDAY

Bivie called yesterday morning and asked me to come to her house on Friday to make our tapes. I feel a great relief. I don't want to even think about *why* I feel relieved.

She said she was trying to decide whether or not to go on with more chemo through a catheter. She wondered if there was any point to going on with treatment.

She said Greg had asked her to teach him how she makes her chili. This pleased her.

They all went to the mall on the weekend. Greg and the girls had frozen yogurts and she had water. Sara piped up, "When do I get to have a stepmother?" Bivie said she was glad Sara had asked. She feels Sara has a positive concept of "stepmother"—Bivie herself being a stepmother to Greg's three older girls. Bivie told Sara that after she was gone, she hoped Daddy would find someone to love him and to help him care for her.

Later she asked Greg if he thought he could manage taking care of the children. He said, "Yes, I'll just have to change—not lie around reading so much, figure out a system for laundry." His pragmatic answers reassured her. She wants to line up a sitter now, so Livia's care will be continuous. All sensible concerns, sensible solutions.

After Bivie's phone call, I met Nikki and other volunteers at noon for lunch at the Golden China. Mrs. Chen's face was round and cheerful. Nikki's face was long and sad and tired. Her red hair seemed faded. We kept circling back to Bivie through the chatter. Everyone was sympathetic. Nikki needed hugs. And Bivie? I think she needs her composure more than hugs.

"God is in the details," said Mies van der Rohe. How many cans of kidney beans, what brand of chili powder, how many teaspoons?

MARCH 9, SATURDAY

Yesterday, at 10:00 A.M., I was supposed to meet Bivie at the Front Royal Conservation Center out on Route 522 South. She told me to come to Gate 2 and she would drive down in her car and show me the way through the compound to her house. However, at nine she called and said she had no car. She told me she would walk down to the gate and meet me. I asked her how far it was from her house to the gate. "About a mile or so," she said. "But it's downhill." I suggested she give me directions from the gate to her house. We argued briefly about this.

"Do you *want* to walk?" I demanded.

"I can manage," she countered.

"Bivie," I said, "I can follow directions. If I get lost, I'll ask someone."

She relented and gave me directions: through the main gate,

up the hill, bear right, turn left at the barns, keep going up, left again at the old dormitories.

Then she asked me if I would drive her to Warren Memorial to have the chemo catheter implanted. She had asked her oncologist if he was doing this just because he didn't know what else to do. "Some people insist on being treated all the way to the end," she told me. I wonder where she got that. But the doctor had told her this new chemo had a 30 percent chance. "It will go directly to my liver," she said. I don't understand this. It's going into her vein. How would it know to go directly to the liver?

We talked about the pain. She said, "You think you can deal with pain, but this is different. It's constant. It's always there, even under the morphine. It doesn't go away. I didn't think it would be like this."

"What's the worst part of it?" I asked.

There was a silence. When she answered, she was weeping. "The worst part is knowing it's never going to go away."

I found her house without any difficulty. She came out her doorway as I drove up. The light was clear and thin, the ground springy. It was just warm enough to be able to smell manure in the dooryard beds Greg had already turned over. She apologized for the stink. They had ordered seeds. "What flowers do you want?" he had asked her.

Her black hair was drawn back into a ponytail, clipped with a red and yellow dragon borrowed from her daughter. It was a playful barrette with a handmade look. Her face gave me a jolt. She was wearing a bright mask of cosmetic paint, skillfully applied and high-fashion, but at odds with her sweatpants and her loose batik shirt. She might have been an actress emerging from a theater's back door wearing street clothes and stage makeup. She also looked bigger than I remembered. A large woman with a very "pregnant" front. Had her cancer really grown that much in a month?

She gave me a tour of her house. She had wonderful, fanciful things in it. In the little entrance vestibule that served as a TV room, she had a collection of '40s toys on shelves over a wicker love seat from her parent's porch. Her daughter's heels had chipped the wicker's white paint; Greg's mother had covered the love seat's pillows in contrasting chintzes: yellow with red cabbage roses; black with pink cabbage roses; splashes of apple green in both. In the long hallway, a framed collection of French zoological prints—hand-tinted a couple centuries ago. On a kitchen shelf thick with generations of white paint, a line of blue and white art deco era pitchers caught the light from a high window above the sink.

A neighbor in the compound had sent a bouquet of roses. Bivie had put them on the oak dinning table. Pink and yellow and mauve roses in a tall vase decorated with a large, loopy mauve ribbon. "Easter colors," she said. She was touched by the gift, but also didn't quite know what to make of it. Would they send bouquets like that to her funeral? That's what I would have wondered. Or was she thinking about the Resurrection? "They saw that the stone had been rolled back . . . ?"

I touched a mauve rose. "Somehow they don't look real," I said. I sniffed. It was real.

She praised the gift again. I agreed sincerely: yes, it was a wonderful gift. She seemed easier about it now. I would allow a mauve rose. Later, in the car, we talked about pansies and violets and how they used to be embroidered on cambric handkerchiefs when we were children.

She kept exclaiming how dirty the house was. She pointed to the kitchen floor, the moldings. To see any dirt, I would have had to put on my glasses, but in the hallway and their bedroom, there were stacks of brown cardboard boxes. They had moved from Alexandria in October and before she could unpack, she discovered she had cancer. I remarked that the house, a '20s sort of bungalow, suited her things. "Yes," she said.

The compound was originally built as an Army Remount Station. All the buildings are cream stucco with red tile roofs. Bivie's house sits above the old stables, which now shelter endangered species. The house is one story and has high windows, like an old schoolhouse. She likes the views: to the east, red tile roofs against a sharp blue sky; to the west, the worn mountain ridges, taupe-colored and nudging hazy clouds. Then below her doorstep, the steep, fenced slopes of blond winter grass where rare deer and antelope graze. "It's beautiful up here when the snow falls," she said. She described a monochromatic landscape, a soft shifting of grays.

In the ER waiting room we sat on a leatherette bench by the elevator where a TV was mounted high on the wall above us. I pulled out my tape recorder and I asked her about the girls, when they were born, what she remembered, how she met Greg—all good, happy stuff punctuated by the hospital's paging system, elevator doors, echoing footsteps. I haven't had enough nerve yet to rewind and see if it "took." It was a slightly stilted interview. If we hadn't been making this tape for her daughters, for posterity, it would have been more of an exchange. I would have told her about my children too. We would have had a conversation. But I kept thinking: they aren't going to be interested in my babies—this is for them. So there was always a slight question in Bivie's manner—Is this what you want?—as if something was missing—which of course it was.

Then they put us in a curtained booth. Bivie sat on the table and I stood beside her. We went on taping. Various technicians would part the curtains and cheerily ask, "Well, why are you here?" Their faces would fall when she told them, "I'm here for a chemo cath. I have cancer."

"Is that hard?" I asked her. "Seeing their faces fall like that?"

The question interested her. She considered it without answering it.

Finally Jack Landis showed up for the surgery. I hadn't realized that he was the one who had done her colostomy. I grumbled that he'd kept us waiting almost an hour and he grumbled back. Sue Reid assisted him. Our children had gone to school together. We talked about what they were up to. Neither Jack nor Sue asked what I was doing there. But at one point, Sue said to Bivie and me, "I bet you two make a good team."

This pleased me. "Absolutely!" I said.

The two of them had a patter like stand-up comics. Jack made sick-o gags, Sue protested and groaned. He wisecracked about keeping Bivie's breast out of the way, about her blood squirting out, about blotching the procedure, about his belly getting in the way. All the time his hands moved so deftly and lightly that they might have belonged to someone else. They snipped, mopped, threaded the catheter into her vein just below her collar bone. Beside him, Sue kept a firm hand on Bivie's left breast. On the other side of the table, Bivie and I held hands. Hers was surprisingly warm and small, with stubby, pink-painted fingernails. The table was tilting her head down. Wisecracks came out of her mouth too—she sassed Jack as good as she got—but her dark eyes were open wide. She looked like a painted child. She kept holding onto my hand.

Later, as we walked out, she thanked me.

I said, "Well, it would be kind of dreary to go through that by yourself."

"I would have been fine," she argued. She told me how she'd driven herself to the hospital during a miscarriage between the girls. She could manage. As if to prove it, on the way home, she corrected my driving. "Pass that guy," she'd instruct. "Get in the other lane." I was reminded of driving with Agnes (Andy's mother). I couldn't help smiling.

We talked about the clothes she would wear on her cruise, about her hair, my hair, about pieces of jewelry we'd been given.

Her weight distressed her. "On my chart," she told Sue, "they've written, 'obese, thirty-nine-year-old female'."

"Oh, that's just a clinical term," Sue said breezily. "Morbidly obese is what they worry about. That's when you get all sorts of health problems. I mean we're talking three hundred pounds and more."

"I used to be able to wear a sixteen," Bivie said in the car. "Now it's Lane Bryant." This disgusted her. She likes clothes, has taste, used to enjoy shopping for quality bargains. She showed me a wallet-size picture of herself. Not at all fat. And very pretty.

Bivie, who besides being a food manager, a kindergarten teacher, had also been a cosmetologist, offered, "I'd love to do a makeup for you!" And when I confessed that I hated to shop but liked nice clothes, she said, "Oh, I'll take you shopping!" The sun was warm through the car window. It seemed a wonderful, luxurious idea. A wave of her wand, a couple hundred dollars, I am remade! I fantasized about eating a good, long lunch with her in the kind of upscale restaurant that attracts women who shop in heels.

When we stopped outside her bungalow, she didn't seem to want to get out of the car. I felt like I was on a first date: What now? Is this the right thing to say? Did I blow it? Do we kiss or shake hands? Do I say thanks for the nice time?

Amazingly, it was a nice time. But I didn't tell her. I kept my voice businesslike. "I'll call you Sunday or Monday." Maybe I said it ten times. I gave her leg a pat. I sensed an awkwardness, and love.

Now I think that maybe her reluctance to get out of the car wasn't so much waiting for something I wasn't giving her, but a "back to reality" dread. The drive home had been an escape. Open the door and what waited? Chemo, nausea, pain. God knows what waited.

Later that afternoon she was going over to Winchester to have a pump connected to the little hose poking out above her breast. Jack had taped it flat against her skin. A nurse had come into the booth with a tray of tape and swabs and gauze to show her how to clean around the incision, what kind of bandages to use. Now she had two hoses to keep clean, one to pump in poison and one to take out shit. What bothered her most about this new hose was Jack's order to keep the incision dry. This meant giving up her showers. Another piece of the fruit.

At home that night, in the kitchen, making lasagna with Andy, I remarked how hard it must be for Bivie to be repelled by her body (the way I so often am by mine) and at the same time to face the prospect of letting it go.

"It's the only one you've got," Andy commented wryly.

Odi et amo. Do men have this ambivalence about their bodies?

Morgan complained, "Mom, why are you doing this?"

"I'm not thinking about the why," I retorted. "I'm just in it and trying to get through."

The hero mom. But this isn't true. The *why* does bother me. Am I doing this out of curiosity? I talk with my friend Theresa.

She suggests with humor that maybe Bivie is my midlife crisis. It seems as good an explanation as any.

I think: Maybe by the summer it will be over. Then I think: How can I want it to end?

MARCH 12, TUESDAY

Saw Bivie this morning. Took her a fringed piano shawl to wear on her cruise. It belonged to Andy's grandmother: a tablecloth-size square of peach-colored silk embroidered with pink roses and green leaves. Bivie was very pleased. She'd sail in vintage style. She draped it around her shoulders and the fringe swung above her bare ankles. I was reminded of Renoir. "I've got the figure, all right," she said sharply.

She showed me her pearls, plump and lustrous in a slender velvet box. Greg had given them to her. She held an antique crystal earring up to her earlobe. It flashed softly in the tawny daylight from her shaded bedroom windows. She showed me art deco slices of carnelian embedded with arcs of tiny, aged rhinestones that had lost their spark. She showed me a Victorian chain of small garnet beads, a rope of oblong freshwater pearls, a necklace of turquoise dots and silver threads—all very delicate, very feminine, very old-fashioned.

I asked her about the layout of her bungalow. It struck me as peculiar. A dining room and kitchen took up one end of the house. Bivie and Greg's spacious, high-windowed bedroom took up the other. They were connected by a long hallway. The girls' bedrooms were off this corridor, but there was no living room. "Oh," Bivie explained, "this house used to be the infirmary." She raised an ironic eyebrow.

I met her sister Linda who was there to help out. The three of us were sitting around the dining-room table talking when the phone rang. Linda answered it, hesitated, then covered the receiver with her hand. "It's for the 'lady of the house,' " Linda told her sister. A sales call. Bivie took it. She listened. Her face hardened. "I've already got that taken care of," she said into the phone. She said it several times, her voice sharper each time. Finally she hung up. She looked at us. Behind the annoyance in her eyes, there was doubt.

"Was that a woman selling grave plots?" I asked.

"How did you know?"

"She got me a couple weeks ago." The woman had been amazingly aggressive. I had asked someone about her (one of the advantages of small-town living). Before pushing graves on the phone, she had sold used cars.

Bivie wasn't amused by this absurdity, but her face unpinched slightly. "She must have been going through the phone book," she decided wearily. The call was not an omen after all.

Bivie was worried. Only four days after starting the new chemo, she had blisters in her mouth. She showed me the implanted catheter. The skin under the transparent plastic bandage was red and itching—a reaction to the plastic, she thought. She was also concerned by the yellow and purple bruising around the incision. I said it looked to me like a natural enough consequence of the surgery. She had an appointment with her doctor in Winchester that afternoon. Could I pick up her morphine?

I carried it around in my purse all afternoon. I worried about being robbed by drug addicts. After I taught my evening class, I drove back up there to deliver it. The house was dark. She was watching television with the girls. Greg wasn't home. She thanked me for the morphine.

I asked her what the doctor had said about her blisters. She said he had discontinued her chemo drip. "He said if I kept going on it, in two days I wouldn't be able to swallow," she told me.

She was stoic, but it must have been a blow. Half a day used up getting the catheter in, the soreness around the incision, the itching under the tape, the nuisance of keeping it clean, the loss of showers—to no avail.

We agreed to meet when she got back from her cruise.

MARCH 21, THURSDAY

It snowed last week, a fast, wet fall that barely covered the leaves on the floor of the woods but outlined all the gray trunks and branches against the gray sky. The only color was the yellow blobs of my daffodils scattered among the snow-coated oak leaves, their dark edges lifting under the white. It reminded me of one of Bivie's Victorian engravings, call it "Woods in Spring Snow," with the daffodils hand-colored too brightly—undiluted dabs of chrome yellow on stems colored blue-green over the black ink.

After Bivie left on her cruise, I felt freer. I was able to focus on my work, to pick up a murder mystery after supper and read about invented deaths.

Perhaps the appeal of fictional murders is that there is always a cause to point to. There is always a bad guy who "dun it" (and whose mother was probably at fault). There's a reason for the warped personality, for the evil. Reasons are satisfying. But with Bivie, how can I point to a reason? How I can say: your death comes because (1) You ignored the warning of your father's death from the same cancer, and (2) You ignored the bleeding while pregnant with Livia—wrote it off as hemorrhoids.

This is not satisfying. Nor is it true. Even if she'd paid attention, she might not have been able to prevent it. Earlier discovery might only have served to prevent her from having the baby.

Bivie herself theorizes that perhaps her pregnancy had kept the cancer at bay.

I have occasional spasms of nervousness. I'm eight years older than Bivie. My children are virtually grown. I'm where she's bargaining to get to. I've made an appointment for a pelvic, a Pap smear, a mammogram.

MARCH 28, THURSDAY

Yesterday a postcard in the mail from Jamaica:

Cheers! Everything has been perfect so far (except me unfortunately), Greg has been great about letting me set the pace (snail's). The first two days we mainly slept—we *both* needed the rest. The colors are incredible and the people friendly— Hope this makes sense—I'm on drugs—Love Biv

On the front, blue sky, turquoise water, white high-rises on a rim of white sand, a fuchsia cascade of bougainvillea.

Called her this morning to say welcome back. Her voice was, as usual, sleepy and very far away when she picked up the phone. She said she couldn't talk to me now and would call back—probably not that day. We hung up without any pleasantries. I thought: *She doesn't want to talk to me.*

APRIL 2, TUESDAY

A long (half hour) talk with Bivie on the phone this morning. Her voice weak and tired throughout the conversation. Usually after the first minute, she perks up and you can't tell from her voice that she's sick. "Did your cruise work out?" I asked.

"No," she said, her voice flat and depressed. She had been in pain the whole time. She had to force herself to do things—even getting up for a meal was a problem. She said it was a long way to the sun deck from her cabin—maybe she managed it once or twice. Mostly she stayed in her room. She said she managed to write two postcards—one to me. Greg wrote the others for her. "He's a saint the way he puts up with me," she said.

"He loves you," I told her. "You'd do the same for him or your sister and think nothing of it."

But there I was correcting her feelings, trying to persuade away her guilt, her frustration—instead of acknowledging it like I'm supposed to.

She talked a lot about a fight she'd had with Sara last night. While Bivie and Greg were away on their cruise, Greg's parents had moved into the house to take care of Olivia, but Sara had stayed with relatives in D.C. Now she was delighted to be back home. Bivie, however, was feeling too bad to put her to bed. She asked Greg to do it. Greg told Sara to turn the TV off, but there happened to be five minutes left of Sara's favorite show. Sara had a tantrum. "Why did you leave me? You don't love me!" she howled at Bivie. Greg was annoyed at Bivie. ("Make up your mind. You told me to put her to bed. Now you say she can finish the program.") Bivie tried to get up and take over but couldn't. She is only pain-free when she doesn't move. "You're always feeling bad!" Sara accused her.

Bivie is back on another chemo. The doctor won't give up, it seems. She's going to see him tomorrow. We agreed I'd come see her Friday.

We talked about day care for Livia. "We ought to get it straightened out in the next couple months," I said. "Next couple weeks," she corrected me. "I'm not going to be able to take care of them much longer."

She talked about being goal-oriented and feeling that she was wasting time. So many visitors, who took up time, but if she didn't see them, she just lay there, unable to do the things she wanted.

"Such as?" I asked.

She wanted to get her bedroom in order. (I see it in my mind's eye—the unmade bed, rumpled sheets, the expanse of bare floor littered with unpacked boxes, clothes, pictures, books, shades drawn and an amber light coming through. Feminine chaos, a lifetime of possessions unsorted out.) She said her sister was coming and would help with that.

She was also frustrated by not being able to keep a journal. We talked about making another tape.

"Anything else?" I asked.

"Oh sure. I want to be a movie star."

"Oh?" I said.

"I'm just kidding," she said.

I asked her how she felt about making a video for hospice volunteers. She was interested. I said we'd talk more about it.

Then after I hung up, out of the blue, one of the calls I'd made about day care paid off. A friend's sister called to say she could take Livia along with her own toddler. I called Bivie back and gave her the number. Greg had a possibility lined up as well.

APRIL 4, THURSDAY

Nikki called last night. Bivie's in the hospital at Winchester for pain control. Nikki found her so doped up that she could hardly speak. Nikki talked about the changes in her. A fine down all over her face. And a change in "affect"—flat voice, I think she meant.

Nikki was angry. She said she doesn't cry for her patients

anymore. She's not sure that's good. But often she dreams about them when it gets close to the end.

APRIL 5, FRIDAY

Called Bivie in the hospital. Her voice was drugged. She complained about sleeping all the time. Caroline, at my behest, had been to see her to ask official permission to film an interview with her. Meanwhile, I'd gotten a pair of filmmakers lined up to make the movie. I was up about this, but Bivie was skeptical. She was concerned about costs. I told her it wasn't going to cost her anything, that the expenses were our responsibility.

"How much?" she insisted.

"Around five hundred a minute," I told her.

"I can't put a burden like that on my family," she said decisively.

"Look," I argued, "you're the movie star. The star doesn't pay for the film. You're giving *us* something. I'll get the money for it. I'll write a grant—whatever."

She was reluctant to believe it—as if she wasn't worth five hundred dollars a minute.

"Caroline says you still look beautiful," I coaxed lightly.

"She said I looked like you," she retorted.

So we went back and forth doing our mutual admiration dance for a bit. I told her she reminded me of one of the women in Renoir's *The Luncheon of the Boating Party*.

"I love that painting," she said wistfully. And it was as if we were both sitting there in the Philips Gallery, in that lovely paneled room, on the bench in front of *The Luncheon of the Boating Party*, contemplating it together.

"Have sweet dreams," I told her, and it sounded as if she might, at least for that particular doze.

APRIL 9, TUESDAY

Talked to Bivie briefly last night. She's still in a lot of pain. She was discharged from Winchester Medical Center on Saturday, then on Sunday night, the pain got so bad that Greg had to take her into the ER at Warren Memorial to have her medication adjusted. She wasn't up for doing any filming. The filmmakers have agreed to standby but I wonder if we'll actually get to do it.

Greg wasn't home. I told Bivie I'd work with him on the day-care business instead of bugging her. There was a lot of background noise—people coping with kids' bedtimes, it sounded like. It was nine. Bivie was calling out instructions, still "managing" through her pain.

Talked to Nikki this morning. She didn't go out to see Bivie yesterday. The doctor has sent in a Home Health nurse and Nikki doesn't want to interfere. But she thinks Bivie is in for a long, painful struggle. She wonders if the family can cope. "She might die in the hospital," Nikki said. She makes it sound like a second-best kind of death. I wonder if it matters where she dies.

I think of what Nikki said about not crying anymore and what an EMT friend told me about getting "hardened" after a while and I want that to happen to me. I don't see it as a bad thing—as a loss of sensitivity. I see it as gaining strength. I think of a green shaft hardened by fire. I want all the *sap* in me to dry up. I'm tired of feeling watery.

APRIL 10, WEDNESDAY NIGHT

Talked to Greg. He picked up the phone and I said "Greg?" and he said "Yes," and I told him who I was and he sounded as if I'd just passed him a ball and he was fumbling it. So I said I had some information for him on day care and there was relief in his voice.

Practical matters he can handle. We talked for about a half hour. Actually, I did most of the talking. But he seemed tuned into what's happening. There was no protest, no argument when, in talking about day care, I said "after she dies" or "before she dies."

He had just found a new tenant for their house in Alexandria. This pleased him.

He told me that noise bothers her.

"And light?" I asked.

"Yes."

"I wonder if that's the morphine," I said.

"She doesn't like taking drugs," Greg said. "She gets confused. She talks about 'puppies'. We don't have any puppies." In the ER on Sunday night, she kept hearing the noise of the compound's electric gate opening and closing. It upset her.

I told him to try to listen for the emotional content, not to write her off because she was confused. I told him the hospice story of the dying man who was very anxious about his "ticket." This was a man who had traveled a great deal in his business. Finally the hospice nurse got his wife to tell him, "Where you are going, you don't need a ticket." This calmed him. He stopped thrashing around and relaxed. Of course the end of the story is, he died peacefully an hour later. But I didn't tell the punch line to Greg.

APRIL 11, THURSDAY

Ghosts seem to be surfacing. In the locker room at Crooked Run after my workout, I was just about to leave when in walked this woman and I almost gasped aloud. She looked like my sister Mercy might have looked had she not been lost at sea a dozen years ago. This woman was about the right age, early thirties, with the same blonde-brown hair parted in the middle and hanging down, crinkled on either side. She had the same dark eyes and was about the same size (I'd forgotten that Mercy was shorter than the rest of us). I stood there with my mouth open and my gear bag in my hand. The woman put her bag down on a bench by the wall, turned her back to me, and started to undress. There was no way I could look at her without going up and sticking my face under her armpit. I waited around, hoping she'd turn around, but she didn't, so I left.

At home, I looked at the picture over my desk of Mercy scowling into the camera and saw that really, the woman wasn't the same, the nose was different, the shape of her face different. Nonetheless, I can't help feeling that in "taking on" Bivie, I have unwittingly ventured into a Virgilian twilight zone—an underground landscape where my own shades pop across the famous river for a flash visit. I wonder, would Mercy's shade have been so insistent if we had had her body to bury?

I begin to understand why, when a volunteer suffers the loss of someone close, hospice waits a year before assigning another patient.

APRIL 12, FRIDAY

Talked to Nikki this morning on the phone about my notion of getting hardened. (Look Ma, am I doing good?)

"Well," she countered, "I still cry for my patients. I had a patient die this week and I'd been taking care of her for eighteen months. I spent a whole day crying for her!" She laughed. Then she added, "Don't be afraid to love."

Other tips from Nikki:
1. Use the word "change"—as in "I'm seeing changes in you" rather than "You look worse," or "You look closer to the end." Change. A strong neutral word.

2. Don't be afraid to ask questions. Patients can answer or not, their choice. Probing is okay. It can be a part of listening.

3. Medical: She said Bivie's confusion is probably not due to morphine (which is now being pumped into her instead of chemo). She thinks even though Bivie is getting maximum amounts, she is big enough to sustain it and stay mentally clear. She said the confusion might be caused by brain mets—or toxins released by disease.

Thus armed, I called Greg who was off work, then drove over to see him and Bivie at noon. It was a beautiful sunny day. The roof tiles were earth-red against a blue sky, the redbud was blooming pink, the wheat-colored grass was beginning to green. The shades were drawn in Bivie's room. There were silver cracks of daylight around the edges of the shades. The interior of the room was as dim as a brown paper bag. There was less clutter. Some of the boxes had disappeared. The king-size bed was made up with dark red sheets. Bivie's face looked pale and small against her crimson pillowcase. Her family was noisy in the background (which was maybe why it seemed so quiet in the bedroom). Greg and I perched on straight-backed chairs next to the bed, like we were at Sunday school, and Bivie sat up on the side of the bed, enormous as a goddess hung with tubes and pumps and straps, belly swollen, breasts huge in a red tank top and navy shorts. Her skin was hot to touch.

We talked about a lot of things. Greg didn't say much, but his listening was articulate. He knew exactly what was happening to her. I felt a sense of peace in the room and a very sad, quiet kind of love—as if the three of us were sitting at the still point of the universe. When I left, Bivie and I hugged each other with great tenderness and I had to wonder if I'd see her again.

We talked about the kids. Livie's birthday was on Saturday. Bivie was planning to make a cake. Sara was asking "good" questions, Bivie said approvingly.

We talked about her father's death. He had died a year ago Wednesday. "I keep thinking about the way he died," she said. "I wonder if it's going to be like that for me."

"What was it like?" I asked.

"You know, *'Do not go gently'*."

"You mean he died raging? He was angry?"

"They had to strap him down—restrain him."

I couldn't tell her that her death wouldn't be like that. But she said that he had gone along on a plateau with his disease (same as hers, colon cancer), then plummeted and was dead in two weeks. A stoic man, Greg said—as if to suggest he had denied his symptoms until it got so bad he had to give in.

"Is that how you see your disease?" I asked.

"No," she said. "I've known about it longer—since October. Mine has been more like a gradual slide."

I drew a slanting line with my hand.

"Yes," she agreed.

"What do you need?" I asked her.

"A couple days like my old self."

I resolved to talk to Nikki. Maybe they could do something for her with medication. (But there isn't. She's getting it all, Nikki tells me tonight. "She may not get her couple days like her old self," Nikki says.)

To Greg: "What do you need?"

The question disarmed him. "Oh," he said. He shrugged. "I'm okay. I think I've got all the bills under control now."

Now and again he would reach out and shyly take her hand. I could see his gestures pleased her, but she didn't allow herself to respond. Perhaps because I was there. Or maybe she didn't want to open a floodgate.

We talked more about the business of day care.

We talked about her pain.

We talked about the hospice video. She perked up at this.

I met Greg's parents and a sister. They came into Bivie's bed-room, a cheerful group returned from some outing. Dorothy, Greg's mother, went over to the window and raised the shade partway up. I remembered sitting with my friend Mark when he was dying. I kept opening the shades and he kept telling me to shut them. I wasn't comfortable shutting out the sunlight. But now, five years later, sitting with Bivie, the darkened room seemed appropriate.

"Oh you look better today!" Dorothy exclaimed to Bivie. "I love to see the light in your eyes!"

I peered at Bivie and amazingly her dark eyes were sparkling. She'd turned it on for them. But in the wash of light from the window, I could also see that her skin was sallow.

Greg's sister, Nancy, talked about getting her hair done. I chatted about skiing with Dorothy and Keith, Greg's father. Then they moved off. Bivie let out a sigh as if all their brightness had tired her out. She'd already let go of permanents and skiing. Now she all she wanted was to feel decent for a couple of days.

We also talked about her confusion. "Greg says you get con-fused?" I asked.

"Oh yes," she admitted easily. "I have these long conversa-tions with myself. I say something and don't realize that I'm talk-ing out loud."

"Is this scary—or what?"

The question surprised her. She hadn't thought about evalu-ating this symptom. It simply happened.

APRIL 13, SATURDAY

Last night I dreamed about her. I was in an attic, arranging things, and Bivie was there—just a head, no body. She was a doll's head floating around in the darkness under the eaves. She looked younger, pale without the sallowness, and her thick dark hair had been cut in a chin-length bob. There was nothing frightening about the dream and upon waking, the image seemed appropriate. She was about to be "disembodied." She was confined to her head now.

In the dream, her eyes had been sad and wistful. She had talked about separating from her body. Some aspect of it bothered her. I wish I could remember her words. I feel like a student who's dozed off and missed a strategic piece of a lecture. A stab of guilt. And the realization that I could fail the test.

Nikki called this morning. She feels there's still some denial: Bivie needed to be told several times that the darkness of her urine was due to toxins from the liver.

Bivie was cool, detached with her. "I represent the medical profession," Nikki observed. "There's some anger in that direction—which is okay." We wondered if Bivie had opened up to the Home Health nurse, Cheryl.

Nikki did have a "good" talk with Greg who told her that Bivie and he wanted to have it happen at home. This was a breakthrough in communication. Nikki had been thinking Greg couldn't cope, that Bivie would die in the hospital.

Talked with my friend Theresa. She proposed another theory of hospice work: We open ourselves to other people's pain to vaccinate ourselves—to induce a low-grade flu that will keep away the Real Thing. I like it!

APRIL 14, SUNDAY AFTERNOON

I talk on the phone with a board member. We go over plans for
Bivie's movie—just in case she's up to it. We talk about death as
a surrendering. She tells me a story about a salt doll at the beach.
The doll wades into the water and dissolves. I don't get it.

Then Nikki calls. She had gone out to see Bivie and ended
up putting her back in the hospital in Winchester. She was dehy-
drated and in pain. Nikki is going to see her again tonight and
wash her hair for her.

APRIL 15, MONDAY

Met Nikki for a long lunch at Palace Cafe. She had washed
Bivie's hair (still beautifully thick), and found a lace-trimmed
hospital gown for her. "She ought to have something lacy!"
Nikki said.

Bivie was worried about the money for medical supplies
(cleansing pads for her pump, dressings, etc.). She's nickel-and-
diming her own death. So Nikki found a big bag of supplies—
more than she would ever use—and brought them up to her.
Nikki showed her a pad. "This is for cleaning your you-know-
what," she said.

"I haven't got one left," Bivie said.

Nikki wasn't sure what she meant. Did she mean she's gotten
so big she can no longer bend over and see herself? Or was she
talking about giving up sex?

Another loss.

APRIL 16, TUESDAY

Talked to Greg's mom, Dorothy, on the phone. She said that neither she nor her husband were comfortable with Bivie's decision
to die at home. "I've never taken care of even a scratch," she said.
"My husband was a veterinarian—he took care of all that. His
mother died at home and I think he's never gotten over it."

Greg quietly insists, "Whatever Bivie wants."

I went to see Bivie in Winchester Medical Center before my
evening class. Nikki and I went up from the hospice office
together. The room was pleasantly done in teal blue with maroon
accents—more motel than hospital. There was a couch under the
window. The Levelor blinds were closed. She was cranked up in
the bed, dozing. She looked nine months pregnant and shock-
ingly yellow—almost banana-colored. The whites of her eyes
were yellow, too. Her black hair was thick and shiny, shot with
white. She had sprouted a delicate beard of white down on her
chin and cheeks. It looked bizarre but not unfeminine. Her lips
were blue-green.

It turned out to be dye. "I had a blueberry popsicle," she
explained. Her teeth were blue also.

Nikki was relieved. "We worry about blue lips in this place!"
she said.

Nikki massaged her feet. Her toes were puffed like sausages
about to burst in a frying pan. Bivie thanked her for "making an
executive decision" to put her in the hospital, and Nikki felt
better. She'd been worrying about it since Sunday. She said
Bivie had cried. She hadn't exactly chosen to go, but she had
made it clear she wanted help with her pain. Her tongue was so
swollen, Nikki said, that she couldn't swallow more than a cup
of water a day.

Bivie said she was comfortable now. She had switched from
morphine to methadone and a bunch of other medications,
which seemed to help.

"You look very peaceful," I told her. "Not a line in your face."

"Oh, thank you," she said. She seemed pleased. Nikki com-
plimented her on her gown—teal satin edged with maroon, and
said how it matched the decor. She permitted Nikki that compliment, but just barely.

My hands were cold. She liked the coldness. I stroked her
forehead and face while Nikki finished up putting lotion on her
feet. "Be careful going to the bathroom. Your feet are slippery,"
Nikki warned. Her voice was still crisp, but her face had gone
wonderfully soft. As she rubbed Bivie's puffed-up feet, Nikki
glowed.

I sat on the side of the bed holding Bivie's hand. Now and
then she squeezed back hard, like she was sending me an urgent,
secret message. I stroked her forearm, her fingers. Her swollen
skin was stretched as smooth as yellow gold. I could see no hairs
on her arm. My own hand looked very white and wrinkled. I saw
the scattering of fine hairs and freckles, the map of veins, green-
ish blue under the skin, and the lapis ring Andy had given me—
deep blue in an Oriental silver frill. It was loose on my finger. My
hand looked old enough for a granny's.

Livia had started day care, Bivie told us. It seemed to be
working out.

"How are things with Greg?" I asked.

She said she wanted to see him alone. I gathered he'd been
coming in surrounded by family.

"I think maybe we aren't going to get to do our movie," I said.

"Maybe not," she said.

She told a long story, somewhat mischievously, about Greg's
parents, Dorothy and Keith, coming to visit after she had moved
in with Greg. Bivie kept nudging Greg to make the big announce-

ment, that she was his roommate, but Greg stayed mum. Finally, Dorothy went out to shop for something and Keith took Greg upstairs. He picked up Bivie's curling iron and asked his son, "Since when did you start using this?"

We laugh. Then Bivie turned serious. "Whatever difficulties we had in the beginning, my mother-in-law has loved me as if I were her own." Her eyes were solemn, wanting to convince me.

"Yes," I assure her. "I can see that."

Her conversation was fragmented. Every few sentences, she took a breath and tripped out. She visited kindergarten, saw three loaves of bread on the bed, heard a dog barking. Then a second or two later, she came back to the exact place she left off.

I told her there was nothing wrong with her thought process, even if she spaced out in between sentences, in between breaths.

"That's good," she said. Then her eyes rolled up. All I could see was a yellow sliver. A pulse in her neck quivered. She took a shallow breath and was home again, trailing odds and ends from somewhere else in her mind.

She talked about her father. The last time she'd talked about him to me, it had been obviously painful for her. She had had difficulty remembering and expressing. This time, however, she went freely into detail, talking about his pain, how he kept wanting to get out of bed at the end, how they had to strap him down, how someone there had unstrapped him and he had fallen. She moved into gentler memories of his dying. She told how before he went into a coma, she spent the night in a reclining chair in his room. "He kept needing ice chips or water through the night—the way I do," she interjected wryly. "He didn't want to bother me for it, but I wanted him to bother me. Then after I gave it to him, he said good night to me. I lay down in the chair and he tucked me in with his voice. He called me all my baby names. Boo, Biv, Bobo. It broke my heart."

"How sad," I said.

"No," she corrected me. "It broke my heart." She patted her heart. "You know what I mean?"

I nodded.

After we left, Nikki said, "If she'd been talking *to* him, then I would have said it was real close."

I called Greg and told him that Bivie wanted to see him alone. That she liked to be stroked. I told her how Nikki had massaged her feet and I had stroked her arm. He said little. He sounded choked up.

On the way home, it struck me that Bivie had not talked at all about her mother. The whole time I'd known her, she's spoken very little of her, though before the cruise, she showed me photographs of her—a vivacious, pretty woman wearing dark lipstick and cheesing it up for the camera. Bivie also showed me a satin nightgown that had been part of her mother's trousseau. It would have fit an eleven-year-old.

Summers, her mother used to pack Bivie and the older girls off to her grandmother's on the Jersey shore. Her grandmother was Czechoslovakian and used to make ethnic pastries for them. I can't remember what sort. Bivie remembered gorging on them and coming home with the seams bursting on her dresses. Had her petite mother scolded?

APRIL 17, WEDNESDAY

Stopped in to see Bivie before hospice meeting. This time she seemed more removed. Or I was. Now I could see the fine black hairs on her yellow arm. The circles under her eyes gave her a racoonish look. Her feet were still as swollen as balloons with toes painted on. She was wearing a blue satin robe edged with lace. "Sara's favorite," she said. She mimicked Sara's little girl voice: "Mommy, can I wear it when I grow up?" Then she gave me an ironic smile.

"Do you remember the nightgown you showed me that was part of your mother's trousseau?" I asked. But she said nothing of her mother.

"What kind of pastries did your grandmother used to make for you?" I asked.

A smile lit up her face. "Donuts with prune filling," she said.

"How did your visit with Greg go last night?"

"Oh, all right." Her voice was dull. Then she asked. "Do you have trouble talking to your husband?"

The question startled me. I said, "Well, he's kind of like Greg. He doesn't talk about his emotions much."

She nodded and sighed a little.

I asked her how she felt about going home. She didn't answer. I said, "You seem pretty comfortable here. I know hospitals are noisy, but it seems pretty quiet right now."

"Oh, it gets noisy," she said. She took a breath. Her eyes fluttered. She returned. "But here I can ignore it."

I wonder how much her wish for a home death is to save Greg the hospital bills.

Once during the visit, she jerked her head toward the door and in a very sharp, annoyed voice, snapped out some command. Then she realized what was happening and shook her head. "I thought Liv was playing with the door," she apologized. "She's really something else."

I stroked her forehead, then kissed her good-bye.

It was hard seeing her two days in a row. How much harder for Greg?

Later, talking to him on the phone, I said, "How did it go for you last night?"

"Great," he said happily. "We had a real good visit. We got to talk and I massaged her feet for her."

He said they were talking about sending her home today or tomorrow.

I said that his mother had told me that she wasn't up for a home death.

"Well," he explained, "she feels Bivie's going to need some-one-round-the-clock. I'm going to start getting shifts organized. Some of my coworkers have volunteered. My sister is a nurse and she'll come to help out." He seemed on top of it.

APRIL 18, THURSDAY MORNING

Talked to Bivie's sister Sharon on the phone. She's visiting till Monday. She told me Bivie's death would be easier than their father's "because Bivie has already accepted God into her heart. He owes her a peaceful death," she predicted confidently.

APRIL 20, SATURDAY

Talked to Greg last night. He's brought Bivie home. He's got a shift schedule worked out for her care for the next nine days. He said she fell in the bathroom. Talking to Nikki this morning, we thought perhaps her fall wasn't altogether bad. Perhaps it would help her accept her increasing need for help.

I drive over there at two. It's cold and gray out. The dogwood is bridal in the wet woods. The compound's damp tile roofs are almost brown—the deepest burnt sienna against an oyster-colored mist. Along the entrance drive, purple-leafed fruit trees bloom pink. The grass beneath them looks impossibly green.

Turns out Bivie fell in the bathroom at the *hospital*—not at home. "I hate to tell you this, but I fell." Her face is shadowy in the darkened bedroom. She sounds guilty and ashamed. She says

Nikki had told her not to go by herself. She was naked when she fell and didn't want to call anyone. She lay on the floor for fifteen minutes before she managed to get herself up.

She tells me this while sitting bolt upright on the side of the bed, hung with all her apparatus, her eyes closed as if sleeping. Her posture makes me uncomfortable. I try stroking her back, a light touch. "How does that feel?" I ask.

"It hurts," she says.

She lies back and lets me massage her feet for her. We don't talk much. I ask her how it is to be home. She says it's okay. Except for the noise. The noise of the children bothers her. "It's my noise," she says again.

She dozes off. I sit in the little straight-backed chair by her bed and watch her breathe and frown and miss a beat and breathe again. I sit there with her and think and feel not much of anything.

Her sister Sharon spends a long time in the john putting on elaborate makeup. She emerges with lavender eyes and wings of blusher over the matte finish on her cheekbones. Thanks to a curling iron, her bangs curl up off her forehead as if surprised. Sharon is a big woman, like Bivie. She talks about their father's death. She had been there with Bivie. She says he was in a coma, struggling to breathe, and she had "released him." She told him that she and Bivie were okay, that he could go.

Sharon and I sit on the sofa in the dining room. She tells me she has things she wants to say to Bivie but she has found it too hard.

"Things about how you feel about her?" I ask.

"About heaven," she says. "I want to tell her about it." She goes on to say that Jesus is going to meet Bivie and take her through the River of Life and that she will be healed in the waters and given a new body and then He will take her to a marbled-hall mansion where she will see her mother and father again. Sharon told this to Sara. "She was really happy to hear it," Sharon says.

Oh dear. If there's any kind of afterlife, I hope it's something larger than a family reunion in marble halls.

Meanwhile, Sara is contentedly watching *Cinderella* on the VCR—the story of a girl whose mother dies.

Sharon is worried that Bivie (Vivian, she calls her) will die without her. "When?" she asks in a hushed tone, as if the question is forbidden.

"I don't know," I say sincerely. "Two days or two weeks. It may depend on when she decides to let go." I tell her to just go sit with Bivie and be quiet, to open her heart, pray, whatever she needs to do, so that if she isn't here when Bivie dies, she will feel she's *been* with her and not just running around taking care of food and the kids. I tell her she will find a way to talk about what she needs to, but to listen very carefully, and if Bivie doesn't want to talk about it, she will let Sharon know. "It may be something she already knows and doesn't want to talk about," I say.

Sharon says earnestly, "I would give up my life for Bivie's. I would willingly take her place. I don't have a husband. I don't have any children. It'd be fine for me to go."

APRIL 23, TUESDAY

Saw Bivie this afternoon. Dorothy was there taking care of Livia, of the laundry. Bivie was sitting in a chair at her dining-room table. She had pulled a lime-green velour bathrobe across her enormous middle. Her black hair was fluffy and clean, her face still yellow, her eyes still rolling back in her head. She sat with her knees apart, swollen feet planted on the rug, arm heavily on the table, fingers limp (the pink paint on her nails chipped). Her downy chin tilted up as if she were about to snore. She is a

Cezanne now, solid, ungainly, resigned. She might be waiting in a doctor's office dozing off, or in a bus depot. She's been waiting all night, for days, forever.

When I'm at home I think, *Let's get it over with, let's be done with it.* But when I'm with her, time doesn't matter anymore. It's as though I've stepped into her own peculiar warp. I sit and watch her, chat when she comes home, then watch some more, memorizing the planes of her face in the gray spring daylight. No hurry. She confuses words: America for Miracle. She mumbles. It's an effort to make the words come out clearly. On the table there is a potted hibiscus blooming floppy, wonderfully red flowers. We admire them.

"One would look good against your hair," I tell her.

She plucks off a dead one. It is twisted into a soft vegetable cocoon. She plays with it lazily. Then with a shrug of resignation, she drops it into a plastic cup of milk in front of her. She pushes the cup aside. "It didn't taste right," she says. "So I put some cornflakes in it. Now I'm eating cornflakes for lunch. That's all I can manage." She sounds vaguely amused by it. She works her tongue around her teeth. "They get stuck in my teeth," she apologizes.

"Are you comfortable sitting up?" I ask. I'm not comfortable seeing her sitting up.

"Not really," she says. She gets up slowly, goes into the kitchen, forgets why she's there.

"Maybe a glass of water," I suggest.

"Yes," she says. She picks up a glass out of the sink, but fills it down the hall in the bathroom. She sits on the side of her bed. There are roses on the sheets and a pink duvet. Then she lies down.

I rub her feet, one after the other. They are so swollen. The skin is as tight as a drum and the flesh underneath is hard, unyielding. Her toes (nails painted pink to match her fingernails) are a bit softer than her foot.

She looks very relaxed and peaceful. The light coming through the old shades is kind. I stroke her forearm. No swelling. It looks thinner than last time, the skin is looser. I notice that her cheeks have sunken slightly. She is losing weight around the edges of her cancer. The mass of it occupies the middle of her. We hold hands. She squeezes mine. I squeeze back. I stroke her forehead with the side of my crooked forefinger, draw the planes of her face. Her silvery down on her cheek feels as silky as baby hair. With the tips of my fingers, I draw lines back through her hair.

Then we just sit there. I notice the old prints of butterflies on the opposite wall. "I hadn't noticed your butterflies before," I tell her.

She rolls her head on the pillow toward them.

"Did you know that butterflies are a symbol of hospice?" I ask.

She is interested.

"The change from one form of life to another," I explain. "Caterpillar to butterfly."

The room is very quiet. I hear her inhale. "I'll take that with me," she tells me.

I sit there. Then I promise, "Bivie, whenever I see butterflies zipping around my flowers, I will think of you."

She nods.

I look at the butterflies on the wall. "What color would you be?"

She rolls her head again toward them. "Purple blue."

It fits.

I sit there a bit longer. The numbers on the clock don't mean anything—a foreign language. Then I have the feeling I should go. I tell her. I stand up and kiss her forehead and tell her I love her. Then I say—and I had rehearsed this in my mind, but it comes out naturally—"I'm going to go up to New York for a couple days. If you decide to go while I'm gone, have a safe passage."

"Thank you."

Or maybe: "I will."

I don't remember. I walk out into the corridor, and my eyes are stinging. I talk to Dorothy instead of crying.

APRIL 26, FRIDAY, NYC

I keep seeing the red hibiscus, her yellow cheek in the slant of daylight, the way her feet were planted on the rug as if they would be enduring forever. Unbidden, these images boomerang back, crash into my mind with hallucinogenic clarity. I walk crosstown on Forty-first for a meeting, ride a bus up Broadway, and *zoom*, I'm assaulted by a sharp-edged, two-dimensional, intensely red hibiscus skimming across the top of my brain. An unsettling, upsetting effect. There's probably a name for it. But not what I expected in terms of grief: no tears, no well of emotion. Just zoom, boom, then ping—it's gone and I'm left wondering if I'm going nuts.

MAY 1, WEDNESDAY

Bivie died last night. I'm going to try to get this down in order. I got back from New York on Saturday evening and talked to Nikki. Bivie was still alive and still at home. Nikki had gone out there that afternoon with Helen Zebarth, a founding mother of our hospice and an RN. They went to talk to the children about what was happening to their mother. But Sara was off somewhere playing and no one seemed to know exactly where. So they talked with Greg about the girls, and also with Dorothy, Greg's mother, who is still worried about having Bivie die at home. Helen insisted that it was Greg and Bivie's decision and whatever they decided, Dorothy would have to put up with it.

Sunday night about 10:00 P.M., I got a call from Dorothy. They were having problems controlling Bivie's pain. Her pump wasn't working. (Later I learned that Bivie's younger sister Betty, desperate to help, had been punching buttons on the pump and inadvertently locked it.) Greg had been taught how to work the pump, but he wasn't there and wouldn't be back for an hour. I told Dorothy I'd call the hospice nurse for her. Nikki was out of town at a hospice conference, but Mary Jane Lee was on call. I got her right away. However, Bivie's pump was under the jurisdiction of Home Health. Mary Jane didn't know how to reprogram it and even if she had been familiar with that particular type of pump, she would not have been able to change medication. Moreover, the Home Health nurse on call was reluctant to drive out there—a forty-five minute trip. She told Dorothy to wait for Greg. We were all phoning back and forth. I offered to go out, but Mary Jane said there was nothing I could do. It was a matter of pain control. "It doesn't sound like she's about to die," Mary Jane reassured me. "Her hands and feet are still warm." I was not very reassured. Bivie's pain was the issue, not whether I missed the moment of her death.

Early the next morning, a Monday, I call the house and get Cheryl, the assigned Home Health nurse. Bivie and Greg had been up all night. Greg had unlocked the pump, but the Home Health nurse on call had not returned his calls, and he had been unable to increase the dose and make her comfortable. All night she sat bolt upright on the edge of bed. Greg woke every twenty minutes to punch in an allowed extra "bolus" (dose).

Cheryl sounded upset over the phone. She had upped Bivie's medication, but without apparent effect. She wanted to call an ambulance and admit Bivie to the hospital.

I asked her, "You know that Bivie wants to die at home? She and Greg have discussed it and decided that she wants to be at home."

"No," Cheryl said. "I didn't know that." She sounded a bit shocked. I asked where Greg was. She said he wasn't there but would be back shortly. So I told her she had to run it by him before she called an ambulance for Bivie. I told her I'd be there in half an hour and not to do anything till I got there and we could talk. So I went in torn jeans, not stopping to change.

Betty, Bivie's sister from Florida, met me at the door. She was large—considerably bigger than Bivie. Betty was wearing a halter top and denim skirt and the expanse of her skin was tan. She had a husky voice, a slow smile, and worried hazel eyes. I walked into the bedroom and there was Bivie sitting on the side of the bed, legs on the floor (but not as firmly as when she'd sat in the chair). Her shoulders were slumped, her head tilted back slightly to breathe, her eyes were closed. She looked exhausted.

Cheryl, a pretty woman in red lipstick and a white coat, sat beside her on the bed with one arm around her shoulders. Cheryl had a stethoscope hanging around her neck, but her sensitive face was as pained as Bivie's. The side of the bed sagged under the two of them. Every light in the room was on. Dorothy was there, hovering anxiously.

Impulsively, I went right to Bivie and kissed her forehead. She didn't open her eyes. I told her it was me. "You're having a rough time, aren't you?" I said. And she seemed to relax a bit. (How much of this I'm revising in the telling I don't know. Looking back, it seems that as we went through Bivie's death together, everyone of us interpreted various events according to our needs—a kind of involuntary instant rewrite.) Anyway, Bivie lay back on the bed. Cheryl seemed amazed. Perhaps it was simply the pain medication finally kicking in. Or perhaps when I came in, Bivie felt she could relinquish control.

We discussed the situation as Bivie lay there flat out on the bed, breathing noisily and shallowly. I would have liked to pull her up onto some pillows to ease her breathing, but was afraid to disturb her sleep. Betty sprawled on the bed beside her, almost booming: "My sister should die at home. It's her last wish. The hospital is cold and clinical."

Dorothy, little and neat and tidy, objected quietly, "It's *not* her *last* wish."

"Not yet, anyway," I said to Betty.

Clearly Dorothy, who had been managing the show, felt she couldn't cope any longer. She had no nursing skills, was frightened of Bivie's pain and the unknown physical side of her death. The nurse—I don't know. She seemed paralyzed by her sympathy. Bivie hadn't peed for something like twelve hours, and Cheryl talked about catheterizing her, but didn't do it.

Dorothy was becoming sharp with Betty and Betty kept booming and the nurse had an anxious voice.

"We shouldn't be discussing *this* in front of her," Betty pronounced. She raised her eyebrow like a mother talking over the head of a child.

"Don't be silly," Dorothy snapped back. "She knows she's dying."

I told Betty that Bivie had been very open in talking about her death. "I think it's okay to talk about it in her presence," I said. Betty backed off momentarily.

Then it got fiercer, and it was making me feel cross and angry, so finally I said: "There's a lot of anxiety in your voices. I really think it would be best if you discussed this out of the room so Bivie can rest."

To my surprise, the nurse and Dorothy left gratefully. Betty stayed. I turned out the lights, stroked Bivie's hand, rubbed her feet—the routine. She seemed out. Betty was hostile toward Dorothy: "She wants it *her* way. She's trying to control it all."

In an attempt to defuse the situation, I told Betty to stay with Bivie while Dorothy and I talked. (Somewhere in there, the nurse left, after a long conference on the phone with Mary Jane.) While Dorothy and I were out of the room, Betty managed to get Bivie on the pot beside the bed. The fact that Betty managed it some-what eased Dorothy's anxiety. Betty is very strong. She hefted and coaxed Bivie in a loud voice: "Come on baby, I'm here for you. I'm here for you, Stinky." She was a bit freaked by the color of the urine. "Come and look!" she said, panicking for a moment, "It's dark brown!" I remembered Nikki talking about her urine and said, "That's the way it's been. It's normal. It's her liver."

Betty didn't say: "What do you mean?" So I didn't have to admit my ignorance.

While this was going on, Dorothy and I talked in the dining room. She said that it was Bivie who wanted to die at home and Greg was just going along with it, because he wanted whatever she wanted.

"And you're the one holding the bag," I said. "They decide this, but then it ends up in your hands."

This seemed a relief to her. She started to weep, and I hugged her. I felt that was maybe a bit uncomfortable for her. Like Bivie, she wasn't about to go soft.

We talked about getting more support for her. I suggested shifts of friends. She didn't want to involve them at this late date. I asked about Greg. "It's best that he keep going to work," she said protectively. We talked about hiring nurses and the expense of it. She conceded that with a catheter and a hospital bed, she might be able to cope a bit longer. Then she made a phone call and heard that her daughter Kristin, an ICU nurse, was on her way from Los Angeles. The relief was so great, she found it hard to speak. With Kristin there, she felt that they might manage after all.

Betty bossed Bivie onto the pot a second time, but Bivie clearly had problems getting off it. She couldn't get her arms down to grasp the arm rests and help push herself up. She kept banging her back against the back of the chair. Betty finally got her on her feet. Then Betty remembered she hadn't wiped her sister. She started spinning out on this while Bivie wobbled there between us, Betty holding her in front, me steadying her from behind. I was thinking, *For heaven's sake, let her drip dry*. But I was worried she'd fall, so to appease Betty, I grabbed a handful of toilet paper from the dresser and stuck it between Bivie's legs, reaching in from behind, and was surprised by a warm spill of bright yellow urine on the paper and my hand. Anyway, it was the only thing that made me squeamish through this whole business. The stunning intimacy of its warmth. And the irrational fear of being infected by it. I washed my hands, meticulously soaping each finger. It was clear she wasn't going to be able to manage the pot much longer.

I left her sleeping. The house was quiet.

The next day, Tuesday, I went over before my evening class. Going out to my car, I saw a big hawk circling overhead in the woods. The bird's huge, dark wings sliced the air above the new leaves. It kept circling. I thought, *Maybe that's Bivie. Maybe she's gone*. Then I thought of all the times while my friend Mark was dying that I'd seen omens and none of them had been on target. My premonitory tingles had no link at all to what was actually going on.

At the house, Greg and I passed each other in the hallway. He was going to work. His eyes were red. The doctor had come by to see Bivie. He had told them it wouldn't be long.

The hospital bed had come. Trout's Drugstore had delivered it and set it up at the far end of her bedroom. The bed, with its pull-up sides, was a relief to the family. Bivie had become restless in the night and rolled off her bed with a great thump that brought everyone running in fright. Now installed in the new bed, catheterized, and rolled up to facilitate her breathing, she seemed beyond any kind of large movement.

The room seemed newly spacious and orderly. The remaining clutter of unpacked boxes and clothes had vanished to make room for the hospital bed. (This had been one of her goals—to get the bedroom straightened out—and now it was done.) Beside the window next to her new bed, there was an aquarium that contained two turtles rustling around behind dirty glass. They were handsome healthy specimens with bumpy whorled shells. In the silvered light, they looked like something out of a Chinese drawing. The window shade was up about a foot. I noticed that along with the fuzz in the hollows of her cheeks, Bivie had white down on her earlobes as well. She breathed with a slight moan and mumbled sometimes. Her hands were clammy—wet, almost, and no longer so hot. There was a fan blowing on her.

I took to Kristin, her sister-in-law, immediately. She seemed eminently competent and full of love for Bivie. Kristin had been up all night with her, grieving with a stethoscope around her neck. Her long hair was tangled, like a Biblical mourner, but her hands were sure and calm. She told me that Bivie had been talking to her father. "Daddy," she'd said. "Daddy."

While we talked quietly beside her, Bivie started mumbling. We leaned close, straining to hear. Then she said, very clearly, "Mama."

Kristin and I looked at each other.

More mumbling. Kristin took her blood pressure. It was falling.

Betty was trying to feed Bivie cubes of red Jell-O. "Come on, honey. Open your mouth, Vivian. Com'on Stinky, just one more bite." Desperately, she thrust the spoon in between Bivie's teeth. I turned my head away. I heard Kristin tell Betty kindly, "I don't think she needs that now." Betty left the room, choking back a sob.

Betty booms, wanting to be heard, to make contact. But like a foghorn, the effect is "Keep Away." I tried hugging her, stroking her arm, her tanned shoulder (she was wearing an off-the-shoulder white knit top). But it was like stroking the arm of a stiff sofa. No yielding, no response at all. I wondered, Will they write me off as the mad hospice hugger? *My God, the woman just wouldn't leave, went around hugging us all the time, as if we didn't have enough to put up with.*

So I left.

Then, after class (my last one) I went back to Bivie's. It was about seven-thirty and still not dark outside. I drove east on 166 with the late sun glinting in my rearview mirror. To go or not to go.

I've done my bit, I thought. You don't want to push. But then I'd told Kristin I'd stop by on the way home.

I drove up through the gates. It seemed a fine evening to die. The sky was deepening. The stucco on the sides of the buildings had a golden cast. The cherry trees along the drive were almost done blooming and the maples made deep shadows on the fresh grass beneath them.

There were a lot of cars parked outside the bungalow. A man with a pencil-thin mustache and plaid shirt hovered by the doorway looking miserable. This was Bob, Linda's fiancé. Linda, another sister—I'd met her before the cruise. As I came in, she was getting Livia into her pj's. Sara was in the hallway, naked and wet and shivering. She'd just gotten out of the bath. Her towel was soaking. Still in my trench coat, I grabbed a towel from the bathroom and knelt down to dry her. She seemed to have gotten lost among the legs of the adults passing up and down the dim, carpeted hallway. She said, "Are you a nurse or a friend?"

I hesitated.

"She's a friend," someone said from above us. Linda maybe.

Sara told me that her mother had thrown up.

It had been frightening for everyone. Bivie had vomited dark fluid—blood, dark bits, bile—whatever. But Sara was especially frightened—perhaps because she saw the adults so alarmed. She kept talking about it.

"What does it make you think of?" I asked.

"That my mother is going to die," she said.

"Yeah," I said. I hugged her. "It must have been scary," I said.

She babbled on about how it looked—the brown, the black bits. She was still shivering. "Can you find a nightgown?" I asked her. She skipped off. I went into the bedroom to see Bivie. Kristin was still beside her. The room was dim. Kristin and I clutched each other. I could smell her sweat. I was really glad to see her. She told me about the vomiting, the dropping blood pressure. She had called the doctor who had offered an ambulance and emergency-room services. She had turned it down, bravely saying no, they wanted to keep her at home.

Bivie's breathing was distressed. She let out a small moan with each exhale. Her lips were parted, her chin up. Again, I was reminded of childbirth. "You're laboring so hard, Biv," I told her. "It won't be long." Her hands were cooling. They were damp and barely warm. I held one hand and with my other arm, held Sara in my lap. I let go of Bivie's hand and combed out Sara's tangled wet hair. After all the snarls were gone, I kept combing it. She wanted to know if I had a little girl. No, I said, but I had two big boys.

What are their names?

I told her.

"Morgan—that sounds like a girl's name," she remarked.

"It's for both."

She wanted my name, first and last. "What do they call you at your school?"

"Professor," I told her. We laughed. Betty across the bed looked impressed. A professor for my sister. I felt only slightly fraudulent.

Sara talked more about the vomit.

Kristin told her that her mother probably felt better after it. "Have you ever thrown up before?"

"Yes." Her voice was reluctant.

"Didn't you feel better afterward?"

She wasn't sure. She kept coming back to the fact her mother was dying and that she didn't want her to.

"You will miss her," I said. "But you won't be alone. There are lots of people to take care of you."

She said something about getting a new stepmother.

I told her that her mother had talked about this. That her mother hoped she would have a new mother someday.

"I don't want a new mother," she said firmly.

"You want your own mom, don't you?" I agreed.

She nodded.

I kept trying to comfort her instead of listening to her. An instinctive reflex. Kristin was the same. She talked about heaven to Sara. How in heaven, Bivie would be with her own mother.

Sara wasn't consoled.

"You will always have the memory of your mother," Kristin said. "That will never die."

I wondered. It seemed more likely that her memory of Bivie would fade beyond recognition. "You will always have your love for your mother," I tried. "And your mother's love for you. It is in your heart. It is there for you whenever you need it."

Kristin and I were both getting teary. Sara went back to the vomit. Something about little brown bumps. Then somehow she got onto bugs and caterpillars. I thought, *My God, caterpillars*.

I asked if she had seen caterpillars turn into butterflies. She wasn't sure. I went on anyway, plowing through her babble, making a little speech. I told her that Bivie and I had talked about caterpillars and butterflies. I told her that her mother's body was like a caterpillar and she was getting ready to leave it and become a butterfly. "She said she was going to be a big blue-purple one," I told Sara.

But she had bounced off my lap, bored with my story. She danced around to the foot of the bed. Then she announced brightly, "I'm going to be a rainbow butterfly."

Kristin and I looked at each other. We couldn't speak.

Sara came back onto my lap. I could feel her spine relaxing against me. Meanwhile, Livia, small and sturdy and determined, was toddling around in her nightgown, climbing the sides of the bed, playing with the pump, splashing in the water in the plastic basin used to bathe Bivie's brow. She picked up Bivie's glass of apple juice, sipped at it through a bent straw, then spilled it on the rug. She opened up a jar of Vaseline on the bedside table. Carefully, she inserted her fingers. Then, reaching through the side bars of the bed, she very gently began stroking the limp inside of Bivie's arm with two greased baby fingers. "Oh look," said Kristin, her voice choking.

Well, it was touching. But I was also annoyed that no one was watching her. Where were Betty and Linda? Sara was on my lap again and I didn't want to give that up. And I thought, how distracting for Bivie. How can you die with your baby climbing over you and your five-year-old chattering nonstop? Finally Olivia spilled water down her front and started to cry and Betty came in and efficiently cleaned her up.

I put Sara down to sleep in her parents' king-size bed. She seemed happy to get between the covers. Bivie was still making moans. Kristin decided to call Home Health and try to up her dose. She got Cheryl but the phone wouldn't reach to the far side of the room where the pump was, so I stood by the bed (and the phone) and relayed instructions, step-by-step, to Kristin. We had to go through it three or four times before we got it straight. Cheryl was anxious. ("Oh, I can hear her!" she exclaimed. "Poor Bivie!") There was also the distraction of Cheryl's thirteen-month-old baby crying at her end of the line and at ours, Olivia climbing over Sara on the bed in an effort to take over the phone from me. The three of us were all protesting and finally Betty came to the rescue and took the wailing Livia away in her arms. I got the instructions relayed, Kristin punched away and actually managed, under all the stress, not only to push the right buttons, but to figure out the system. Cheryl told us to leave the pump off the lock position so Kristin could reprogram the dose as necessary.

Kristin punched in a new dose. She worried about low blood pressure. "The medicine will lower it further," she said. She was concerned about killing Bivie. I told her the goal was pain control. If Bivie died as a result of it—I didn't need to finish the sentence. She nodded. Now Bivie's feet and hands were cold. I remembered what Mary Jane had said about this. We turned off the fan. Dorothy came in, her eyes large, but calm. Kristin and I told her it looked close—that she might go tonight (I was thinking 4:00 A.M.). I said I wanted to stay, if it was all right with them. Dorothy said she wanted me to stay. I called Andy on the phone by the bed and told him where I was. Sara was asleep under the covers.

I told Dorothy that she should get Greg. I said, if he wasn't with her, he might feel bad later. She went off to call him from his zookeeper duties—a mating watch on some mammal. Kristin also talked to Greg on the phone.

It all seemed familiar, summoning the husband, the sense of anticipation, the quick phone call home, the soft lamplight in

the bedroom, the rustle of concerned women moving quietly—
like a home delivery.

Greg came in, a masculine presence. He carried Sara, still
sleeping, from their bed to her own. Then he sat down on the
bench beside Bivie, cried a bit, talked to her a bit. We all moved
back to give him space.

After a while, we settled in together for the duration.
Dorothy and Kristin sat on one side of the bed, Greg sat on the
other, and I stood behind her head. We held her hands and
stroked her forehead. Her breathing seemed to ease up. The drug
seemed to be working. We chatted quietly. Then there was a
silence. Kristin jumped up and put her stethoscope to Bivie's
chest. "She's gone," Kristin said, starting to cry. Greg burst into
tears. Dorothy and I cried too. Kristin, tears streaming down her
face, stroked Bivie's face, unobtrusively pressing her eyes closed.
It was 9:30 P.M.

The next day, Dorothy described the moment of death. She
had been holding Bivie's hand when she felt a jerk. Then she saw
Kristin jump to her feet with her stethoscope and heard her cry,
"Good-bye, Bivie!"

Greg also felt the jerk as he held her hand. Then he saw her
open her eyes and meet his. "You know how her eyes used to
roll back when she opened them?" he said to me. "Well, this
time, they were focused. She looked right at me, as if she recognized me."

I told him that I felt sure she knew he was there, that she had
waited for him to come and be with her, and that she would have
waited hours longer if needed. (Hospice nurses say there is often a
last moment of lucidity. Or is this wishful thinking? Who knows.)

One moment in time and each of us experienced it so differently. Me: as a silence. Greg: a last look. Dorothy: a jerk of the
hand. Kristin: the absence of a heartbeat.

What did Bivie feel?

———————

After some minutes, Kristin told the others. They came in, Betty letting out a great noise of grief, Monica (Bivie's teenage step-daughter) sobbing. Dorothy and I moved into the dining room—the examining room of the old infirmary. Dorothy kept repeating over and over, "It was so peaceful. It was so peaceful. I can't believe how peaceful it was!"

We all kept drifting in and out of the room as if we didn't really believe it. I told Kristin I wanted to help her clean Bivie up, if that was okay with her, and it was. So Greg and I assisted as Kristin unplugged the pump, cut the stitches. I told them how Bivie had wisecracked when they put the catheter in. Hand over hand, Kristin pulled out the catheter to Bivie's bladder—there seemed to be yards of tubing. She left the colostomy bag in place. With a small alcohol pad, she wiped away dark stains of vomit from Bivie's chin, wiped the corners of her eyes. We lifted up her legs, heavy as oak logs, and pulled out the pillows. Greg lifted up her back, which was still warm, and we took off her nightgown. Somehow her breasts didn't seem as dead as her face. We put on a pretty new gown, laced with ribbon and sprigged with small flowers. She looked lovely in it. She had pretty teeth, I saw as Kristen cleaned them with a washcloth. We pulled up the sheet to her chest, straightened it out, tucked her in, stroked her shin-ing black hair. There was a hunk cut out of it. I noticed, but gave it no thought.

In time, the family started calling out the news and in between I called Mary Jane Lee, the doctor, and the funeral home. Bivie had wanted to be cremated. I gave the information to the undertaker on duty who insisted on talking to Greg. I sup-pose he wanted to make sure the call wasn't a hoax. Greg took the call in the bedroom where he sat with her body.

Betty was angry at Bob, her sister Linda's fiancé. He had

taken Linda out for dinner, despite all Betty had cooked (fried chicken, cabbage, corn on the cob, strawberry shortcake). Because of "Bob's selfishness," Linda had missed "being there"— though Betty herself was out of the room. Betty called Linda's apartment in Alexandria and left a message for them—this despite the fact that they had just gone into town for supper.

"Don't leave a message on the machine that Bivie's dead," I ordered Betty. "Just tell them to call you." She stood there holding the phone to her ear, struggling with her anger. She did as I asked.

Keith, Greg's father, arrived and went into the bedroom to sit with Greg.

There was a question of whether to wake up Sara so she could say good-bye to her mother before the undertakers came, or whether to take her to the funeral home the next day. Since Bivie wasn't going to be embalmed or prepared for a viewing, Kristin and I felt that it would be better for her to see her mother dead in her own bedroom than pulled out of a drawer at a mortuary. So Greg lifted Sara out of her bed and carried her in to say good-bye to Bivie, but Sara wouldn't wake up. Kristin and Dorothy tried a cold washcloth on her face, but that didn't work, so they put her back to bed.

"She just wouldn't wake up," Dorothy said. She sounded a little uncertain. Should they have tried harder? I said, "Well, that solves it then. You tried and she didn't wake up. You can tell her about it in the morning."

After more phone calls and tears and visits to the bedroom, things began to lighten up. We sat in the dining room and the Petersons told stories about tracing their roots, looking for ancestors in graveyards—a hobby for them. It seemed appropriate to be talking about family trees—a kind of continuing life.

Then Betty said that she had cut locks of Bivie's hair—one for each sister, but that Linda didn't want one. Linda, by this time, had gotten back from dinner with Bob. Bob was not in good shape. Clearly there was more going on for him than the death of his fiancé's sister. He staggered up and down the hallway, weeping, hugging Linda, and finally fell asleep, snoring away on the little wicker sofa in the vestibule. So Betty was really annoyed by his behavior. She felt he was trying to upstage Bivie's death, to focus Linda's attention on himself. She called him "selfish." Dorothy tried to soothe her. Linda said nothing, her face impassive.

Perhaps Betty felt some disapproval in the room as she went on about "locks of my sister's hair." She then announced that she was "not afraid of death" and still had her father's dental plates in her car. "I'm going to have a ring made of them. There's a lot of silver in them. Or maybe it's white gold."

Her announcement reduced us to silence. She glared at Linda. I took a breath and said, "Well, everyone grieves differently." I told them how my father-in-law had died and I'd been given one of his old shirts, which I liked to wear because it made me feel close to him, but that my husband couldn't stand to see me wearing. It jarred him every time he saw it. "It's okay for you to want her hair," I told Betty. "And it's okay for Linda not to want it."

"Are you a psychiatrist?" Monica (Bivie's stepdaughter) demanded quizzically.

Driving home at 1:30 A.M., I felt relief and also a kind of gentle high, as if I'd attended a birth instead of a death. It was a beautiful, navy blue spring night with the moon one day past full. The house was sleeping. I felt a bit like a stranger in it. I sat downstairs and turned the pages of a magazine and drank a glass of wine. When I finally went up to bed, somewhat to my surprise, I had no trouble falling asleep. Andy's breathing was familiar in the dark. I felt cradled, as if being gently rocked by what had happened in Bivie's bedroom. It was like falling asleep at sea.

The next day was sunny and cool. Like a florist's refrigerator, the cool weather had kept all the dogwood blooms in perfect shape. I thought of Bivie in a refrigerated drawer. Nikki went to see her at the funeral home. "For closure," she said.

I called the house and had a nice talk with Kristin. She wanted me to come out and talk with Sara and I said okay, though I wasn't quite sure what there was to talk about. Dorothy had told her about her mother's death when she woke up that morning and she appeared to be fine. Then I talked to Linda and asked how Bob was doing. "He seemed to be having a hard time," I said.

"Here," she said, "talk to him."

So I said, "Hi."

He said "Hi" back.

"How are you doing?"

He mumbled something.

I said, "I feel it's not only Bivie's death that you're dealing with." And he told me a shocking story about the death of a boy-hood friend. At the time they were both sixteen. Bivie's death had brought it all back to him.

As prearranged, I drove over in the late afternoon. After the extraordinary intimacy of the night before, I wasn't sure whether to shake hands or hug them. Maybe swinging singles feel this way the morning after. I offered my hand to Greg and he drew me into a hug.

Dorothy told me they had asked in the obituary for memorial gifts to hospice. She said, "It's not only the money. It will make other people more aware of what you do."

My session with Sara was almost comic. She saw me, and reached up, and I picked her up and gave her hug. She said, "My mother died."

I said, "I know. I was there."

End of conversation.

But Betty was determined. She put Sara in a red wagon lined with white pillows. Sarah was too long for it, but reclined like a child odalisque, pearl bracelet around her wrist, knees (below pastel shorts) bare and bent at varying angles as she rearranged the placement of her feet in the wagon. Thus we set out for a walk. Betty, in a black jersey sundress, pulled Sara in the wagon along the compound's upper roads and I walked along beside them. Clearly Betty wanted Sara and me to start talking to each other. "Honey, tell Christine what happened at school today," Betty prompted. "Baby, tell her what you told those ladies."

"My mother's dead," Sara sung out, not particularly interested.

I picked a daisy and gave it to Sara to distract Betty from our dreadful mission, but she kept hammering away at it. I asked how she was doing. She shook her head. This time her voice was soft and shamed. "They've brought all this food. I've been stuffing myself all day. It's nervousness."

I could think of nothing to say—for once. I knew Betty was diabetic—the same disease that had killed her mother three years before. First her mother, then her father, then her sister. Did she wonder about her turn? I felt badly for her. Perhaps she sensed it. The rest of our walk was quieter. She talked very sensibly about helping to take care of the girls. Then she told me how she was saving a lock of their mother's hair for each of them. She envisioned tying the hair in pretty ribbons. For when they were older.

MAY 3, FRIDAY

Last night, by the time I went to bed, I had lost all the serenity of the night of Bivie's death. It seemed a distant gift. I felt as if I might roll off my side of the mattress into a dark hole. Depression, I diagnosed. Ignore it, I prescribed. Go to sleep.

I'm not sleepy.

That's part of it. Sleep will help.

And it did. Maybe writing everything down isn't such great therapy after all. I spent most of the two days after Bivie's death obsessing into my computer—when I wasn't visiting or on the phone with her family. It seemed very important to *get it down*— as if it all might evaporate and leave me blank. But now that I've put all I can remember into this machine, I don't feel any relief of catharsis. I just feel as if I've corkscrewed further into her dying.

The funeral will be held on Saturday in Alexandria. I told them I wouldn't go—that I was going to see my older son run in a track meet. But I asked if I could come when they buried Bivie's ashes on Sunday.

MAY 6, MONDAY

Spent Saturday watching college kids run at the Mid-Atlantic Championships in Gettysburg. Sunny, cool, green grass, red track. Sitting in the bleachers, I felt as frail as an invalid who is rolled out into the sun after a long illness. Andy and Tim and

Morgan were attentive and relaxed—casual as nurses who knew the patient would mend. Their unspoken caring felt luxurious. The teams of runners all wore bits of colored nylon. It was strange to see so many healthy bodies in so many different shapes. I found it deeply reassuring to watch them run round and round the track. They ran their hearts out. When Morgan placed in the 10,000 meters, I found myself weeping behind my dark glasses.

Coming home, there were notes in the mail from both Caroline and Nikki: it was not only their pats on the head that made me feel good. It was as if they were giving permission for it to be over. Their cards thanked me for a job well done. It is odd to think of Bivie's death as a *job*. And odd to be thanked for something that *happened*.

By Sunday, however, I was feeling more or less normal. I drove over the mountains to Orkney Springs for the burial of Bivie's ashes at Prince of Peace Lutheran Church. I almost didn't recognize Greg in his suit. I wondered if it was the same one Bivie helped him buy for their cruise. The day was overcast and muggy and there were clouds of gnats. The grave was on a hillside behind the church. A plump minister with a comforting, low-key manner said the usual prayers. Bivie's sisters had all gone home— the gathering was mostly Petersons. A young man in shirtsleeves and suspenders carried a shovel as discreetly as was possible. In front of the hole, there was a large arrangement of red and yellow flowers. I didn't stay to watch the dirt get filled in.

I wonder what Bivie's maiden name was.

MAY 9, THURSDAY

Had lunch with Nikki yesterday. Talked mostly about Bivie. Nikki said she was beginning to wonder about that phrase "Death with Dignity." Is it just a hospice fantasy? To me, dignity implies control. But the process of dying is letting go, bit by bit, of self and self-control. Dying with dignity is about as likely as pushing out a baby with dignity: when it gets down to the line, dignity is not an issue. What you want when you have to surrender dignity is a cushion of love. And Bivie did have that. Whatever the conflicts in her family, they were strong enough to give her love.

Talked to Kristin on the phone. She said Bivie's maiden name was Splitgerber.

AUGUST 6, TUESDAY

Bereavement visit to Greg. Sara showed me their pet python, a female named "Stevie" who ate "dead rats." Then Sara brought out the pair of turtles I had seen beside her mother's window the day of her death. They were not clay-colored as I remembered them. They were yellow-spotted. So much for my reporter's sharp eye for detail. What else did I get wrong?

"Leopard turtles," Greg called them. They were land turtles from Africa. Some lived to be a hundred. They'd had them for three years and hoped to keep them alive a long time. Sara told me that when Greg died, she would take care of them, and when she died—well, she was a bit vague on that, but she was definitely into continuity of care.

"What do you remember best about your mom?" I asked her.

Sara's eyes became solemn. "That she loved me," she answered.

I could scarcely believe my ears. Had she been coached? Did it matter?

I want to tell Bivie, "You did it! We did it!" I'm not exactly sure what "it" is. Nonetheless, I feel like celebrating.

SEPTEMBER 29, 1991

Talked to Greg on the phone yesterday evening. He had just come in with a load of groceries and was about to start supper. He said he and the girls were doing "pretty well, pretty well." "I've learned I have to stop whatever I'm doing when they need attention," he said. "I can't just ignore them and keep on cooking. I have to stop and give them a hug or whatever."

Next week he will fly out to Wyoming with his black-footed ferrets and release them into the wild. The girls will go to stay with Dorothy and Keith. Greg said that his parents are adding on to their house in order to better accommodate the family's new needs. Their generosity—though they would not see it as such— moves me.

Told Greg about this journal. He says he would like to read it, but the prospect makes me uneasy. It is one thing to have your wife die on you and another thing to read what someone else has written about it.

I have another misgiving. Bivie was pleased that I was writing about her. I think she felt that she hadn't "made her mark" during her life and that perhaps her death could be a kind of accomplishment that would help others. But reading this over, I see it sets down my own hopes and fears far more clearly than Bivie's. I watched her dying, but knew so little about her! I never *quizzed* her on the life she was giving up.

Talking with her family at various times after her death, I have picked up random details. I was surprised, for example, during a bereavement visit with Greg, when he spoke of Bivie's father as "an abusive man," a demanding tyrant who "belittled" his children.

"But she spoke of him with such love," I objected.

Greg shrugged. "He was her father."

We sat digesting this in silence.

Bivie was a far more complex person than I ever knew. For a short time, I felt intensely close to her. But I was, essentially, a stranger at the end of her life. And I think that this was probably a good thing. If it is good to die in the community of family and friends, it may also be good to have a referee. Whatever my own private agenda, I was not tangled up in the passions of Bivie's life. I could hear Sara more clearly because she was not my five-year-old. I could better understand Dorothy's fears because she was not my mother-in-law. I could be nonjudgmental about Betty's "locks of hair" because she had not cut them off my sister's head.

On the other hand, I cannot say along with the hospice volunteers I interviewed so long ago that being with Bivie was not stressful for me. Her death was indeed peaceful and I believe at that moment, we were all in harmony with it. But I wasn't always at peace with myself. I was anxious about being accepted. I worried about saying and doing the right thing. Perhaps with my next patient, I will feel more secure.

There are things about being with Bivie that I am still trying to sort out. Take the dream I had of her disembodied head. Was it really a dream about her? Or was I dreaming about some aspect of myself?

Then there's the issue of her pain. When I asked Nikki about this, she suggested it was simply the luck of the draw: Bivie had pulled a short straw. Some patients, she said, have virtually no pain at all. But I keep wondering why had we not been able to better control it? Was it a communication problem or a medical problem?

I also wonder what her death would have been like in the hospital. Would it have been as peaceful? Would Sara and Olivia have been able to say their long, inchoate good-byes? Who would have been beside her?

Throughout the summer, I did think of Bivie whenever I saw a butterfly. I saw velvety black ones with blue "eyes" on their wings, zebra-stripped ones, amber-colored monarchs. I watched them carefully as they flitted around the impatiens on our deck. I kept expecting to see a big purple-blue one.

Now the leaves are beginning to turn. I find I cannot tuck the experience of Bivie's death neatly away in a journal. It is not for lack of trying. She has left me a large legacy, unwieldy and mysterious, and I suspect I will be learning from it until it's my own turn to die.

How presumptuous I was at the outset to think I could somehow "help" Bivie die! Ultimately, the process of dying—like the process of living–is a unique and solitary task for each of us. No one can "get it right" for us. On the other hand, we *can* bear witness to each others' passages. At birth and at death, we can hear each other, learn from each other, love each other. And there is the most profound help in that—for everyone present.

1998

AMBER

It may be that some little root of the sacred tree
still lives. Nourish it then, that it may leaf and
bloom and fill with singing birds.

—Black Elk

February was warm, our daffodils came up early. Now it's March and the inevitable freeze has flattened them. They're lying splayed in green circles under the oaks, their bright yellow heads violent-looking on the winter-bleached leaves.

Eight years ago this same time of year, in 1991, Bivie was dying and I wrote about how the same daffodils looked in a wet snow. This morning the new volunteer coordinator at hospice called to ask if I would take on another young mother with two children—boys this time, five and seven, a few years older than Sara and Olivia were at the time. It's been a while since I had a patient, so I said yes. I can't help feeling as if my path has circled back to Bivie, that I'm at another beginning, and that inside the sweep of that seven-year circle, the ghosts of subsequent patients are observing me with sad, patient eyes.

Since Bivie died, I have had fifteen patients. About half I remember only when I happen to drive past the turnoff to their houses. I sat with them once or twice while the caregivers went to the supermarket or the dentist. Usually the patient was asleep or beyond talking. With other patients, however, the connection was deeper. Despite my rituals of closure after their deaths, they remain very much with me. A polite kind of haunting. They do not wake me at night with moans and rattling chains; they point no accusatory fingers. They simply stand in my mind, stoic as Homeric shades, silent and unchanging teachers. I am the one who is restless, full of questions, squirming in my seat. "What happened?" I ask. "What did *that* mean?" They do not answer, they merely persist.

From time to time I bump into Greg Peterson at the supermarket and we hug in the aisles. He seems happy. He has not remarried. I have to wonder, if between his five daughters, his mother, his sisters, he has enough women in his life. He looks no different, but the girls do. Sara is thirteen, tall and willowy, and enjoying a slight celebrity from having had my account of her mother's death published by hospice. Olivia is nine—dark and sturdy, has mischievous eyes and a look about her that recalls Bivie.

Blue Ridge Hospice has also grown—in a great, awkward spurt. We have become licensed by the state, certified by Medicare, approved by insurance companies. In the space of a few years, our budget has expanded from $90,000 to over $1 million. From a paid staff of two, there are now more than twenty employees. We provide more professional services, fill out more forms, obey more regulations. Nikki Hill, Bivie's nurse, is now an administrator. As a volunteer I no longer report to our director; I report to a volunteer coordinator—a position originally funded by one of the grants I wrote.

I no longer write grants, but in the interval since Bivie's death, I have written three murder mysteries, all featuring the same sleuth, a part-time college English teacher who moonlights as a camp cook in Montana. ("She's really you, isn't she?" friends ask.) After the first one was published, I was reluctant to tell patients. It seemed insensitive—if not frivolous. Here I was killing people off for fun and profit (I hoped), and there they were, facing the grim reality of their own deaths. I worried that my interest in violent death would make them nervous. In fact, the only one who was nervous was me. My patients were delighted to learn that I wrote mysteries. I was a diversion from the tedium of coping with disease. They took pleasure in conferring an authorly status upon me and the one time I ventured to explain my lowly rank on the ladder of popular literature, my patient's face fell in disappointment.

In a mystery novel, the writer creates a world in which everything happens for a reason. The reader must be totally satisfied as to the "why." Joyce Carol Oates describes mysteries as an addiction, a kind of fix that dissolves the "malevolent power" of the unknowable. And perhaps there is the link between my taste for murder mysteries and my pull toward hospice work: the drive to know the unknowable.

People ask, "Why do you write mysteries?" and they readily accept my answer, "Because I like them." But I have never been able to come up with a simple answer to the question, "Why are you a hospice volunteer?" Especially when it comes from the patient. "Because I like it," is mystifying, if not offensive. (*What is there to like about my death?*)

Once, at a regular volunteer meeting, the Why-Are-We-Doing-This question was posed and several experienced volunteers answered confidently, "Because I want to give something back." I thought that sounded pretty reasonable. So the next time I was assigned, when the patient's caregiver pulled me aside and asked, "Why do you do this?" I told her: "I feel as if I've been given a lot in my life. I want to give something back. Even the scales, maybe." I smiled.

She looked at me without expression. Did she sniff insincerity in a statement that came not from the heart but the mind? Did she resent the idea of being a pawn in someone else's game of noblesse oblige? Whatever the reason, she decided she could manage without me. Of course it may be egocentric to assume that her choice had anything to do with my answer. Perhaps she simply preferred not to have to deal with yet another stranger. The barrage of new faces in her house must have been bewildering: first an assessment team, then the assigned nurse, per diem nurses, home health aides, a social worker—and me.

"Because I feel drawn to the work." Better, truer. But when I tried this one out, the patient declared with great authority: "God has given you a mission." And that made me so uncomfortable that I never said it again.

Some motives are not for patient consumption. Most obviously, there is the halo factor. This is not much discussed among volunteers; halos are taken for granted, mentioned only in passing and always with irony. At volunteer recognition dinners, for example, tinsel halos are given out as awards. (In my own case, I think I'm less interested in being considered angelic than in being seen as brave. As in: Ah, she goes in where ordinary mortals fear to tread.) There may be pleasure in wearing a halo—be it good-girl gold or brave-girl steel—but I doubt that this particular hospice perk can sustain anyone when it comes down to the nitty-gritty. We need more solid nourishment than good opinion.

For me, a lot of nourishment comes from the companionship with other volunteers and with our nurses. We share a kind of roll-up-your-sleeves, war-zone bond. No one has to apologize for tears of frustration or grief, but in fact, we laugh more than we cry and share an in-house brand of black humor that often flies off over the edge and can easily ricochet into raunchiness. Like halos, bonding is rarely mentioned except at recognition dinners: "It really is a privilege to work with such a wonderful group of people."

What volunteers do talk a lot about is the "selfishness" of the work—and the mysterious sense of having been given a gift. The gifts are intangible, ever-changing, hard to grasp, harder to communicate. But of all true reasons for hanging in there, perhaps the most true is: "Because you will give me a gift. I don't know what it will be. Only that it will be of great value."

MARCH 20, FRIDAY

Yesterday I visited Amber for the first time. According to the paperwork, she is thirty-six years old—three years younger than Bivie was. She has breast cancer that has metastasized to her lungs, liver, and brain. She's been fighting it for several years. After a final radiation treatment in the hospital, she was referred to hospice and sent home. She uses a walker and is taking anti-seizure medication. Despite the medication, given the aggressiveness of her cancer, the oncologist thought the seizures might recur. He instructed that she not be left alone during the day so her husband Wayne requested a volunteer. He is trying to set up a schedule of people to come in and fix lunch for her while he's at work. The intake nurse noted that he "appeared tense and slightly angry during the interview" and that he was worried about what services were available and which his insurance would allow. The nurse also noted that "patient has no spiritual resources."

The new volunteer coordinator asked if I could commit to twice a week—she did not think it was going to be a long-term case. "Let me see how it goes," I said.

I called the house and spoke briefly with both Amber and her husband. They sounded pleasant enough. I have agreed to come Thursdays at 12:30 to fix Amber's lunch and spend the afternoon with her. Wayne gave me detailed directions.

Claire, the nurse assigned to the case, called to welcome me aboard and she too gave me directions. "Ignore the signs," she instructed. "Someone's turned them all around."

They live way out in the county, halfway up a wooded mountain that has been subdivided with roads scarcely wider than a dozer's blade. At every other turn, new split-levels perch on clear-cut patches of hillside. The gravel on the road has been spun off into the ditches by the residents' four-wheel drive vehicles and the mud is as slick as lard under my car's bald tires.

Despite my two sets of directions, I get lost. A thin sun is heating up the car and I start to sweat. I'm over half an hour late, miles away from paved road and my gas gauge is needling close to red. For the first time in my life, I want a cellular phone. The names on the road signs I'm supposed to ignore unnerve me: I drive past Beyond Tomorrow Way and turn up Steps To Heaven Lane feeling as if I'd strayed into a remake of *Pilgrim's Progress*. I stop at a pristine-looking little house with an oval of etched glass set in its new front door. A teenage boy in sweats lets me use the phone and I call my patient.

Amber can't give me directions but she does give me her address. The boy takes my two sets of directions and studies them for what feels like another half hour. Then he puts on his sneakers, gets in his pickup, and leads me up and down, up and down to the correct road. By this time I'm so twitched that I turn in the patient's driveway without stopping to even wave him a thank-you. I realize that I've driven past the house at least once before.

The driveway is a track churned to the consistency of pudding. The yard swarms with toddlers minded by a cheerful young woman who says she and two friends just stopped by for a visit. The house is a weathered plywood cabin standing on concrete block pillars. From the yard, it looks scarcely bigger than a toolshed and the flight of steps leading up to the front door looks precarious. Amber's mother built it in the '70s as a weekend retreat. It must have been one of the first structures in the subdivision.

Inside, the house is more spacious and better-kept than one would suspect from the outside. The plywood walls are stained dark and bright squares of a batik have been tacked over the windows. Remnant sections of carpet have been neatly vacuumed and the throw pillows on the sofa are carefully arranged. The decor brings me back to the '70s: I might be walking back into a tidy hippie's house.

There are two bedrooms and I find Amber in the back one, sitting cross-legged on a double bed, eating a hot lunch of chicken and green beans on a paper plate. The visiting women had warmed it up for her in the microwave. One of them is sitting on the side of the bed talking about Jesus. Amber, however, is more interested in the large TV on the dresser at the end of the bed. She's watching the soaps, volume up.

Her appearance is startling. Under a bowl-cut, orange wig with severe bangs, her skin is grayish. She has a pointy nose set in a round, swollen face and wears large round glasses with plastic frames. Her torso, in a bright pink T-shirt, is a large ball. Is the bloating an effect of her cancer? A reaction to the drugs? On the wall, there's a framed studio photograph of her two little boys grinning against a blue background, but there's no "before" picture of her.

A walker stands next to the bed. Her husband, who works for a contractor, has installed a shiny new white flush toilet under a window and a fiberglass shower stall in what had been a closet. A ruffle-edged curtain hides the stall but the toilet sits out in the open, incongruous in the bedroom. One tabby cat lounges on the bed at her feet, another lies on the floor, next to a electric baseboard heater, licking a jagged stripe of discolored fur on its side. Amber thinks it must have burned itself on the heater. The burn puzzles her, but her voice is flat. Her lack of emotion puzzles me—as does the cat's scorched fur: if the heater was that hot, why did the cat remain lying against it?

I take the armchair beside the bed. The young mothers take turns coming in. They plunk themselves down on her bed and tell her how hard they are praying for her. One of them offers a video about Jesus.

"I'm not sure I'd watch it," Amber says.

"Oh, it's wonderful!" her visitor insists. "I'll bring it next time."

Amber considers the chicken on her plate. Like the cat's scorched coat, the chicken is another puzzle: "Wayne said there wasn't any left," she says to no one in particular.

The women come and go, and in the spaces between, over the noise of the TV, I ask her about her cancer, how she's feeling.

"I don't have any pain, I'm grateful for that," she tells me. But the prospect of another seizure frightens her. She does not want her boys to see her "like that" again. She says that the boys know she does not have long to live; Wayne told them when she was in the hospital. Now the older boy seems to be avoiding her. "And that hurts." But her voice remains flatline.

I ask whether she has any goals.

She wrests her eyes off the TV. "What do you mean?"

"Is there anything you want to do before you—uh, get too sick?"

She doesn't think so.

On the TV, a beautifully muscled man strips off his shirt for a woman with big hair and red lipstick. She is wearing a dark business suit and sitting behind an executive-size desk. The man undoes his belt. "That won't be necessary," says the woman.

The proselytizing mothers leave. Amber gives me her empty plate. I say, "I'm glad your friends showed up. Otherwise you would have been starving."

She corrects me. "They're not my friends. One of them came to the hospital. The other two, I never saw before." She doesn't want their video but at the same time, doesn't want to hurt their feelings by refusing it. She says her mother believed in reincarnation but she doesn't know what she believes in.

I make the bed for her. She gets out of it without help, ignoring the walker. She's wearing tight short-shorts with her pink

T-shirt and under the ball of her torso, her pale legs are long and elegant. Suddenly I can see her as a sexy young woman.

I strip off the blankets and ask if she'd like me to change her sheets. They are striped beige polyester, almost transparent with age.

"They're the only ones I've got."

"Would you like me to pop them in your machine for you? They'd be done by the time I left."

The question disconcerts her. "No, that's okay," she says. "They're clean."

Good going. What makes me think she *has* a clothes washer? There's no mattress pad and the mattress has sagged badly where she's been sitting. I turn the mattress and put on the bottom sheet. The elastic is shot so when I pull one corner taut, another slips off, but she seems satisfied with my effort.

Back in bed, she watches the soaps. Slim, rich women with shiny, thick hair quiver with emotion. They ooze sexuality, seep tragic pain.

During a commercial break, she says, "You're a writer."

"Yes." I tell her about my mysteries. "What about you? Do you like to write?"

"I used to keep a journal. Poured my heart out into it. There was a lot about Wayne in it."

I nod sympathetically.

"I tore it up."

The stark finality of her statement shocks me. "Why?"

"I didn't want my boys to see what I wrote about their father. They don't need to read all that."

On the TV screen, we watch three older women indulging themselves at an afternoon hen party. They wear flowing caftans and recline together on a sumptuous king-size bed. They eat chocolates and talk about men.

"You were asking about my goal?" Amber says.

"Yes?"

"I guess my goal is my poems. I kept my poems. Could you tell if they were any good?"

I hesitate. I suspect that by "good" she means "publishable." I tell her that I don't know much about poetry but I'd love to read them. She reaches under her bed and pulls out a little book with a flowered cover. I take it and open it up. The lined pages are filled with poems carefully copied out in ballpoint. Her handwriting has a childish roundness. It is also back-slanted which gives me a reflexive little buzz of alarm: the nuns who taught me handwriting had been merciless about backward-slanting letters. A back-slanted hand, they promised ominously, was a sure sign of a defective character.

I start reading. The poems are effusions that ramble on for pages. It's hard to concentrate on them with the TV going. There's no punctuation, no rhyme, no sense of any pleasure taken in crafting them. In the language of country music, she wrote of loneliness in her marriage. She wrote an angry letter to a father who had deserted her as a child and whom she could not forgive. She wrote an inconsolable lament about the death of someone called "Scooter." They are raw passionate spills. They are open wounds. But by any literary standard, they are not publishable poems. My heart sinks. I can feel her waiting for my reaction.

I take a breath and look up. "Wow. You've certainly put down some powerful feelings here."

She gazes impassively at me, waiting for more. I flip back through the pages and find a short poem that stands out from the others, a few lines on "How Time Flies." Her circumstance gave it a certain poignancy.

"I like this one," I tell her.

There's a small, unreadable change in her expression. Surprise? Disappointment? "My teacher liked that one too."

"Your teacher?"

"Oh, I wrote that one back in junior high."

"Oh. Well, I can see why she liked it."

"Why?"

I take another breath. "It seems more formed than some of your longer ones. The voice has a bit more perspective. Maybe a kind of tenderness?" I look at her. Her face gives no clue. Am I failing the test? "I don't know," I worry. "I guess it just moved me." I flip several pages and find the bitter letter to her deadbeat dad. I don't feel secure enough to explore that particular wound. I flip some more pages and stop at "Scooter." "Who was Scooter?" I ask.

"He was my cat." She indicates a collection of snapshots taped to a curio cabinet whose shelves are overflowing with small stuffed animals. The photos are sun-faded and in the center of each one is a large, black blob with a pair of eyes.

"He meant a lot to you."

"I loved that cat."

I feel like I'm pulling teeth. I understand she has taken a risk in showing me her poems, and that my reaction is probably not what she hoped for. I sense she wants to be "discovered," to have me whisk off her poems to a publisher. I explain how poems are published: how she would need to read a bunch of poetry journals and decide where she wanted to submit; how she might have to wait six months for a response. "Even if you have the time," I warn, "chances are that you'd get a rejection. It doesn't mean your poems aren't any good. It's a matter of editorial taste and limited space. You'd be competing with hundreds of other poets. Rejection slips aren't much fun. I would think they'd be the last thing you need at this point."

I tell her that one year I collected twenty-three rejection slips: eleven for a novel and the rest for short stories. Only a couple of the stories ever made it into print.

Her face remains impassive but her disappointment is palpable. My suggestion of publishing one of her poems in our hospice newsletter does not appeal.

During a commercial, she runs her fingers through her orange wig. "My hair's not growing back. That bothers me."

"Yes," I say.

She tells me that she gained weight with her boys, and that after they were born, Wayne lost all romantic interest in her. She relates an incident that makes her wonder if he's "going out" on her. "I told him he should get married again, but . . ." her voice trails off.

"You think he's seeing someone now?"

She considers it, then draws herself up like one of the rich women on TV. "I don't think he's that common." She repeats it, pleased with her delivery.

She asks me to look under her bed and find a box of chocolates. I get down on the floor, down on my stomach, and grope under the sagging bed. I fish out a box of chocolate covered cherries, still in cellophane. They are not the ones she wants. I pull out a box of cream-stuffed chocolate rolls. Nope. What she wants are the chocolates someone brought her in the hospital. "They were imported. They had nuts in the center and a kind of truffle filling, but with little flecks of crunch in it. They were *really* delicious." Her voice is wistful. It's the only real emotion I have heard from her during the entire three hours of my visit. "Maybe Wayne threw them out," she speculates, her tone a flatline again.

All the way home, I fantasize about working with her on her poems. I imagine unlocking a buried talent, helping her turn out something wonderful, perhaps a poem to be read aloud at her funeral. I envision a nicely designed, computer-generated booklet of selected poems, a small edition of, say, ten—just enough for her family and a few close friends. I decide that the next time I visit, I will get her to try some left-brained associative exercises.

Then my own right brain kicks in. Maybe she can't hold a pen. Maybe she can't even focus on a page.

That night I dream of Joan.

JOAN

"Then you should say what you mean," the March
Hare went on.

"I do," Alice hastily replied; "at least—at least I
mean what I say—that's the same thing you know."

"Not the same thing a bit!" said the Hatter.

—Lewis Carroll, *Alice in Wonderland*

JOAN is one of the ghosts in my circle: a tall, angular woman in
her late sixties who watches me from under the bill of a Baltimore
Orioles cap. The cap is a lucky cap, a present from a grandchild,
and she wears it with a quilted pale blue bathrobe. She has had a
double mastectomy. Her flat chest and her fearless shoulders—
together with her baseball cap—give her an aura of athletic brav-
ery. In her hand she holds out a silver Christmas tree ball. It is
her gift to me.

I met Joan and her husband Jim, who was retired from the military, in mid-December three years before. They lived in an old
farmhouse they had restored and filled with family photographs
and souvenirs from their travels around the world. We sat down
together at the kitchen table. Jim did not beat around the bush.

While Joan sipped a cup of herbal tea, he laid out for me, in chillingly clinical detail, the progression of his wife's cancer. To my disconcertment, she listened eagerly, as if he were describing something she had accomplished. Now and again she would chime in to correct a date or the name of a drug. They both referred to her death casually, in the way one might mention an appointment with the dentist.

I was having a hard time listening. I drew in a breath, concentrated on opening up to them. Under the table, I uncrossed my legs, let my hands rest palms up on my thighs as if to catch whatever they might toss my way. I maintained eye contact and made appropriate listening noises—all the tricks of the trade. Still, their conversation was making me squirm inwardly. Perhaps I thought they should be more shaken by the prospect of her end. Perhaps I was disconcerted by their cheerful use of the "D" word. Whatever the reason, I was uncomfortable. I glanced distractedly through the doorway into their living room and noticed their Christmas tree, an artificial one, which Joan had decorated with dozens of red bows. There was a silence. And before they could start up again, I filled it with a compliment. "How pretty your tree looks with all those red ribbons on it," I said.

Or at least that's what I intended to say. What came out was, "How pretty your tree looks with all that cancer hanging on it."

I thought: *I did not say that.*

But I *had.* Their eyes widened, their jaws dropped. We stared at each other. Then, like a movie starting up again, Joan took a sip of tea and Jim went right on chatting about her cancer. It was as if I had let out a loud fart and they had politely chosen to ignore it.

I left as soon as I could and drove to the hospice office for a meeting. At that time, I was a member of the board's executive committee and Helen Zebarth, a cofounder of Blue Ridge Hospice, was serving as president. Helen is a RN, a teacher, a woman of great compassion and experience in matters of death and dying. I pulled her aside and blurted out my appalling mistake. I suppose I was hoping for absolution; hoping that she might say, "Oh, don't worry, slips like that happen all the time." At the very least, I hoped for a penance—something I could do to make amends.

But Helen simply stared at me. "Oh, Christine," she said. "That's *bad*."

"Yes, I know," I wailed in despair. "But what can I *do*?"

"Nothing," she said firmly. "You can only make it worse."

So I did nothing. Or at least, I *said* nothing. But I kept bringing them small gifts, a jar of gourmet jelly, pine-scented potpourri, a tin of homemade cookies. "For your Christmas," I would say. They seemed surprised and pleased. Had they forgotten my ghastly faux pas? If not, they appeared to have forgiven me.

I could not, however, forgive myself. The mistake kept pricking me, an old thorn under the skin. Over the years, I told the story to friends, to fellow volunteers. I strung myself up as an object lesson: "It happened because I wasn't listening. Because I was afraid. I was uncomfortable with their talk of death. I focused on my own fear instead of *being with* them."

I still believe this is true. But in the meantime, I've become kinder and gentler to myself and more familiar (if not "comfortable") with the facts of disease and death. So it occurs to me as I write, that perhaps there was a kind of truth in my slip. It is possible that my wandering mind was doing an Emperor's New Clothes shtick, calling it out the way it was. Perhaps Joan and Jim's cheerful chat about cancer was as artificial as their Christmas tree. Perhaps, underneath all the pretty ribbons, they were, in fact, terrified.

MARCH 24, TUESDAY

I check in with Claire, Amber's nurse, on the phone. I'm really happy to hear her voice; under the familiar merry bubbles, there's a strict professionalism I admire and trust. I'm reassured when she says that she finds it hard to connect with Amber.

I think of my friend Katie. Like Amber, she was a young mother and victim of breast cancer. A few days before she died, another friend and I brought her lunch (eggplant parmesan in Styrofoam takeout containers). The three of us ate it together in her living room. Katie was up, dressed, and felt no pain. Her only complaint was that she didn't seem able to feel anything. Beside her on the sofa, there were three diaries she'd been keeping—one for each of her children. She picked up one, then listlessly put it back down. "I keep thinking I should be feeling *something*," she said.

The hospice nurse called it "autism." She explained that during the last stages of dying, there is often an emotional shutdown.

Is Amber's flatline affect a signal that she's close to the end?

Claire thinks not. "If anything, she seems to be getting stronger. Maybe her brain tumor has something to do with it. It might have triggered a ministroke."

"What about depression?"

"She could be clinically depressed," Claire allows.

"Can't you give her some uppers?"

She laughs, a lovely spurt of bubbles.

"No, really. I mean it."

MARCH 26, THURSDAY

Second visit. I call Amber before leaving home and ask if I can pick her up something on my way through town. Groceries? Something from McDonald's? She hesitates. "A chocolate shake would be nice. But I don't have any money right now. Maybe I could pay you later?"

"Let me treat you to one," I offer.

She agrees with some reluctance.

Coltsfoot blooming back in Amber's hollow—first yellow dots of spring in ditches along the road. In Amber's yard, a patch of purple crocus glints in the sun like a scrap of satin finery dropped on bare earth.

Along with the chocolate shake, I bring three picture books from our hospice library. Last visit, she had complained about the religious books the church women had brought for the kids. I offered facts-of-death books for them and she expressed interest in seeing what we had. Mare Rockwood, who wears two hospice hats—social worker and children's bereavement counselor—chose the books for me and I had made the trip over to Winchester to pick them up.

I find Amber in the back bedroom, lounging on top of the bed watching her soaps. She's wearing an olive green tunic, emerald green leggings, and a black turban that looks a bit small for her head. At the back, there's a cobweb of hair, too fine to determine color.

She thanks me for the shake and tells me about the church women. One of them had come back unannounced with a friend—yet another stranger. When they walked into her bedroom, Amber had been dozing on her back, half-naked and without a wig or scarf to cover her bald head. She felt violated and angry but she had not been able to tell them to go away. Instead, the next day she had asked her friend Debby to call them and warn them off. "It's like they're using me, showing me off to each other," she complains.

Brain tumor or not, she's sharp.

I get a closer look at the singed cat this time. I had been wondering if someone had held it against the heater, but as far as I could see, the burn (if that's what caused the jagged, discolored streak of fur) had not gone through to the skin. The cat's name is Miss Muffet. Her mother's cat. "Mother got her in eighty-two," Amber tells me. Her mother had died the following year of ovarian cancer. She had been in her forties, only a few years older than Amber is now. Wayne had been living with them at the time. One morning, after Wayne had gone to work, Amber woke to find her mother had died during the night.

"We didn't know she was that close. She kept everything to herself. Except her pain. She let us know about that all right." Was there an edge of bitterness in her voice? "Her door was locked."

I look at her. "Did she usually lock her door at night?"

"No. I had to break it down. She was lying on top of the bed. She looked real peaceful. She was on her side—like this."

Amber stretches out diagonally across the bed. She lays her hands on the pillow, palm to palm as if in prayer, then lays her cheek down to rest on top of them. She closes her eyes and holds the pose. I have the eerie feeling that she's trying out being dead. I wonder if her mother had died in the same bed.

During the week, I'd located a computer graphics volunteer who was willing to work with Amber in producing a book of her poems. But when I bring up the subject of her poems and offer the volunteer's services, she's not interested. "I've done that," she says, dismissing the idea as if it were ancient history. "I typed them up when I was taking a typing course."

I suggest making a tape of memories for her boys. She doesn't like that idea either.

"I'll help you," I promise. "All you have to do is talk to me like we are now. I'll ask you questions and you can answer them. I'll give you my recorder and you can turn it off whenever you want. It'll be fun."

"I don't think I could do it."

I try to digest her "no" and can't quite. I know that story-telling takes a certain amount of energy, but it also can be liber-ating. Like cleaning out closets, there are discoveries ("I'd forgotten all about that!") and choices ("Save it? Chuck it?"). At the end, one feels at once lighter and stronger, better able to tackle the next job, which, in the case of the patient, may be sur-rendering to the process of death. The formality of making a tape, of moving beyond conversational drift, seems to increase the beneficial effects of the process. (I hesitate to say "healing effects"—the word "healing" has become too fuzzy around the edges for me.) Plus, a tape is a tangible legacy for the patient's family. Plus, it's an easy way for me to connect with the patient. "I'll probably ask you again," I warn her.

She *almost* smiles.

She looks over the children's books I'd brought. Like a business-woman scanning a report, she briskly turns the pages. "These are more for after I'm dead," she decides. She slides them under her bed. I wonder if our library will ever see them again.

What she wants more than any kind of tape or books is a den-tist appointment. "My teeth need a lot of work," she says. "I wish Wayne hadn't put *that* thing in." She indicates the toilet under the window. "I don't need it. He should have saved the money for the dentist."

"Your teeth are bothering you?"

"Yeah," she says vaguely, as she leafs through the yellow pages. She picks up the portable phone on her bed, dials a dentist's office, and makes two appointments for cleaning—one for herself, one for Wayne. "He's never been to the dentist," she tells me after she hangs up. She worries about whether she will be able to climb up into the dentist's chair, but the appointments seem to give her a measure of satisfaction.

To me, it seems a strange sort of end-of-life splurge. I picture a skull in a coffin. The teeth are dotted with new silver fillings.

As before, I remake the bed for her. The same sad sheets. I ask if she would like me to see if hospice has any sheets that would fit her bed. "Sure," she says, frowning. Have I insulted her?

Throughout the entire two-and-a-half hours of my visit, the thirty-inch TV at the end of the bed is blaring soap operas. Amber seems to take a certain relish in my ignorance of who's who and patiently explains the various characters to me. I try to pay attention, but the intense pitch of artificial emotion, the overbright colors sliding across the screen, begins to unhinge me. A couple of times, however, she turns down the volume and cocks her head. "Do you hear that?"

I listen and catch a muted guttural sound, a low gurgling. "Sounds like a pigeon. Or maybe a dove. Is it on your roof?"

"I think it's under the eaves."

I go out into the hallway and stand outside the boys' room looking up at a hatch in the ceiling. The sound is louder.

"I kept hearing it last night," she says. "Wayne said it was just one of the boys making a noise."

"Sounds like a bird to me."

My response gives her a grim satisfaction. "Wayne said it was the heater."

Maybe, I speculate, Wayne hadn't wanted to get out of bed in the middle of the night and cope with a bird in the attic space.

She turns the TV back up. I'm ready to run away. I feel at once drained and overstuffed. For Amber, however, the shows seem to work like a lullaby. She relaxes into a secure sleep.

I make my escape. On the way down the rickety front steps, the family dog, a shepherd-size mongrel, gets to his feet. He's tied to a tree at the bottom of the steps. As I walk by, he cowers as if I were raising a club over his head.

MARCH 27, FRIDAY

Trying to make sense of yesterday's visit, I picked up *Final Gifts*, Maggie Callanan and Patricia Kelly's book on understanding the communications of the dying. They compare death to an uninvited, unwanted visitor—a stranger who takes up more and more space. Certainly Amber is crowding me out of my comfortable routines, just as her soaps crowd me out of her room. She uses the remote to stay in control: with it she can regulate both volume and visitors. Does she wield her own personal remoteness in the same way? Is her lack of affect a power tool or a side effect of her cancer?

At an in-service meeting on pain control, one of our oncologists spoke about the potency of distraction as a painkiller. Soaps as morphine?

We tend to think of dying as high drama. In fact, dying at home of cancer may be pretty boring.

Moreover, for all my attachment to storytelling, some stories may be better untold. No doubt Amber's right to spare her boys her journal entries about their father. But is there *nothing* she wants to save for them?

MARCH 30, MONDAY NIGHT

Claire calls on her cell phone. She says she offered Amber an antidepressant. Amber said she had tried Prozac and didn't like the way it made her feel. She dismissed the idea that she was depressed. Claire suspects some deep-seated psychosis.

I suspect abuse and anger.

Whatever it is, we both sense a darkness—the bear within.

Claire says Amber laughed once—a slight laugh.

"You're doing better than me," I assure her.

"She actually turned down the soaps so I could listen to her heart."

"So you could listen to her heart? I love it."

"You'd be amazed by the number of my patients who are hooked on the soaps. You'd think they'd want something more worthwhile."

"God, it's depressing," I complain into the phone. "Every time I think of her life, it seems so bleak. So empty, so bereft—so poverty-ridden."

"They have that big satellite dish in the yard," Claire observes. "And he drives a big new truck."

"I mean *spiritually*." Even as the word left my lips, I wince. Who am I to judge?

"We're only seeing a piece of it, Christine," Claire chides. "We haven't met the children, or her sister or the friend who comes in to take care of her."

"That's true," I concede.

She lets out a wistful sigh. "I miss Hal."

HAL

Teach us to number our days, that we may apply
our heart unto wisdom.

—Psalm 90

HAL was our previous patient. He was ninety-three years old
and dying of a melanoma on his leg—a consequence, he
believed, of spending his boyhood summers messing around in a
rowboat. "The tops of my thighs were always sunburned," he
told me. "We didn't know about melanomas back then." Now
he was white and frail in body, but his mind was fiercely sharp
and his will indomitable. His first career was as an engineer at
Front Royal's now-defunct rayon plant. After his retirement, he
had become a realtor. As it happened, twenty-five years before,
he had sold my husband and me our land. The coincidence
pleased us both. He remembered the parcel of land. I remembered him: a small, wiry old man who kept his hiking boots in
the trunk of his car. Where younger realtors sat in their cars, he
had pulled out a survey map and marched us around the boundaries.

His wife Babs was a warm, affectionate woman with an
uncertain look in her pretty eyes: she had Alzheimer's. Hal's pri-

mary concern was what would happen to her when he was no longer able to care for her.

I used to drive them to the supermarket and wait in the car with Babs while he shopped. In return, he presented me with the last tomatoes, small, misshapen fruits, from his garden.

When he stopped eating regular food, I made him custards using heavy cream and organic eggs. I had never made custard before, but I followed the instructions in an old copy of *The Joy of Cooking*, and actually felt a thrill of joy when I pulled the little cups out of the oven (their tops picturesquely dusted with nutmeg) and found that the alchemy had worked. Proudly, I put them in a basket, covered them with a blue-and-white checked tea towel, and drove them over to the house feeling like the sainted Marmee visiting the sick in *Little Women*. Hal was almost as pleased with them as I was.

We made several tapes. We sat in his sun-drenched living room, which had a dry, old-book smell that I found pleasant. He sat in a Victorian parlor chair inherited from his mother and behind him, through a large picture window, I could see the hazy September sky and yellow leaves falling from trees he had planted forty years before.

He had been born in Rhode Island; like me, he was a Yankee transplant to a small southern town, and his stories evoked the New England landscape of my own childhood. I could see his stories. It was as if I were visiting my own past along with his. He talked about his mother's vegetable garden, the immigrant Italian children with whom he played, his pet crow and the horse-drawn hearse that carried his grandfather's coffin. (During the funeral procession, the crow escaped and, to the communal horror of the mourners and Hal's own delight, the bird had dive-bombed the undertaker's black silk top hat.)

Babs sat in her customary wing chair and listened with great interest as he recalled their courtship. On the last tape, he delivered a terse tribute to her that he had obviously rehearsed in his mind but had a hard time getting out. I paraphrased what I thought he was saying. "Is that right?" I asked him.

"Yes," he said with relief. He fumbled to turn off the tape and both of us sat in silence blinking away tears. Babs looked a little frightened.

On the admission sheets, Babs was listed as her husband's primary caregiver, but in fact, Hal was *her* caregiver. If she appeared capable, it was because he constantly gave her cues. It was his mind that kept them both afloat. Claire and I worried about how she would cope if Hal suddenly succumbed to a heart attack (a real possibility). Claire tried role-playing with her, asking what she would do if her husband had a fall. Thus Claire discovered that Babs could no longer work the telephone. We were haunted by the picture of her running out of the house and wandering the streets in distress. The weaker Hal became, the more we felt there was a need for a paid caregiver in the house. But Hal kept putting off hiring someone. He refused to admit defeat. Finally, with some anxious nudging from Claire and me, his daughter intervened and engaged a caregiver.

Two days before he died, Claire pinned a holy medal on the lapel of his bathrobe. He showed it to me, knowing that I had been raised a Catholic. "What's it for?" he asked. A member of the Presbyterian church, the medal seemed to make him a little uneasy, but at the same time he did not want to turn any help down. "For protection," I told him. "I had a little gold one I wore as a child. It was the envy of all my Protestant playmates."

He smiled a gently ironic smile.

I leaned in for a closer look at the medal. "There's a picture of

Mary on it. It's a prayer that she will carry you through this like a mother."

With the exception of his declaration of love for Babs (and I don't think he actually used the word "love"), it was the most intimate moment we had shared. Our Yankee souls were both a bit embarrassed by it.

He remained in control up to the last minute. The last afternoon we spent together, he said, "I'm ready to go."

Babs sat up in her chair like an indignant belle. "Oh," she exclaimed, "thanks a lot!"

That evening his legs gave out and he allowed himself to be carried to bed. Babs kissed him good night, pressing her lips hard against the silver fuzz on his skull. "Love you to pieces," she told him and suddenly I saw them as young and flippant and radiant with health.

Twenty-four hours later, he died attended by Babs and their daughter.

Afterward, I dreamed a haiku for Babs:

The ridgetops go first
yellow leaves fall like memories
her mind—bare branches.

I wrote it down in the morning. It seemed familiar. Where had it come from?

Hal's death prompted me to think about my own father who had died a year and some months before. (Hal, in fact, was the first patient I had taken on since my father's death.) Like Hal, my father had been stubborn and controlling. The driving force of his life had been to support and protect his family, but he had little interest in his children as individuals—as long as we stayed "on track." When one of us deviated from his notion of the proper track, he felt duty-bound to rescue us. Consequently, my father and I had a combative relationship until my mid-twenties, when I learned how to sidestep.

Six months before my father died of complications after open-heart surgery, I went home with my tape recorder thinking that perhaps I could kill two birds with one stone: capture in his own words the story of his childhood (rather a mystery for me and my siblings); and in the process, make some kind of open-hearted contact with him. Given the eventuality of his death, I was poised to lower the polite, daughterly shield I'd been carrying for the past thirty years. But when I proposed making an oral history together, he blew up at me—a startling refusal, still unfathomable to me—and I quickly dropped the subject.

It made me wince to think that Hal, in his reserved way, had shown me more affection and approval in the space of two months than my father had shown during the whole of my fifty-odd years. Somehow, through hospice, I had found a connection with a stranger that I had never been able to find with my father. It struck me as pathetic—and, at the same time, quite wonderful.

And now there was Amber.

I wondered if Claire would pin a medal on her at the end. Did she pin holy medals on all her patients?

APRIL 2, THURSDAY

It's been hot for the last week, in the high eighties. In the woods, you can almost hear the sap bubbling. It doesn't even cool off at night. We sleep with the windows open and hear the owls. In town, everyone comments on the heat. There's a communal disappointment in the lack of a leisurely spring; the cool voluptuousness of April is missing.

Today's my day to see Amber. All week I've been feeling fuzzy and depressed. Can't seem to focus on my writing. I have the unpleasant sense of being stuck inside a Plexiglas cylinder—the sun is heating it up, everything outside it is slightly muffled. I'm cut off in some sort of firm, but invisible way.

It occurs to me that being *connected* is as essential as air or food. When there's no current, we start shutting down—a kind of psychic brownout?

I talked to Mare Rockwood about this. She believes that even if you can't *feel* connection, there's still a flow between living beings. As she sees it, I pick up Amber's bleakness and she, perhaps without even being aware of it, absorbs my "light and energy"—in Mare's words. A flattering theory—and comforting—but I'm not sure I buy it. Nonetheless, it makes me think I need to center myself more when I go into her house. I visualize a compact, weighty ball of light in my abdominal cavity, bright ballast in a dark hold. If there's any leakage that benefits her, so much the better.

I'd been trying out a kind of prayer/exhortation recommended by one of our veteran volunteers. He says that every time he goes to visit a patient, he instructs his eyes to see, his ears to listen, his heart to be open. But perhaps I've been seeing and hearing and feeling too much. In this case at least, all the input makes me buzz with questions. I spin with possibilities, feel myself loosening at the edges. What's real? Am I looking at an abusive husband or a paranoid wife?

So what I think I need to do is just try to be there with her without all the busy-ness of perceiving.

As I write this, Claire calls on her cell phone. She sounds frustrated. She had prescribed medicine to flush Amber's port, the tube implanted in her chest for chemo, but no one had picked it up so Claire called Amber to find out why.

"How much does it cost?" Amber asks.

"Six dollars."

She hesitates. "Okay," she tells Claire. "Pick it up and we'll pay you back."

Claire balks. "I've been stiffed too many times," she says.

"My sister's here," Amber tells her. "She'll pay you."

So Claire agrees to get it, drives to the pharmacy, and finds that Wayne has already picked it up. She drives out to the house, but Wayne doesn't show with medicine. Amber says he's picking up a pizza for lunch. So her port remains unflushed. Claire has driven thirty miles for nothing.

She thinks there are lapses in memory—this is one of them?

I drive out. The air-conditioning in my car is broken and I feel cranky. As I told Andy at breakfast, this is the first patient I've ever had whom I haven't looked forward to visiting.

In the hollow, the tangle of brush and briars along the road is veiled with chartreuse bloom. White clouds of wild cherry float among the bare oaks and there's a promising magenta stain on the branches of redbud. I think about Jesus: How nice it would be to able to rely on Him—a column of strength that would protect me against the gloom in Amber's house. At the convent where I went to high school, we used to trade gilt-edged holy cards with a Victorian look: they showed a pale, gentle Jesus in clean pastel robes. The other day, I saw the identical cards for sale in the window of what used to be Trout's Drugstore on Main Street.

In fact, the Jesus I encountered through the nuns was too hungry to be safe. He was insatiable. As with an abusive husband, nothing was ever good enough. He demanded self-punishment from his brides.

At this point in my life, I think I prefer a feminine incarnation of divine light. A Mother Goddess. If God has to be male, I'll take Ganesh, the elephant who breaks off his tusk and wields it like a pen to write out his blessing for humankind. Lord Ganesh, Remover of Obstacles.

Amber is eating pizza when I arrive. The Jesus women have come and gone, leaving her pizza for lunch and two meat loafs, one for tonight, one frozen. Amber tells me they are "real sweet" to do it, but she doesn't want anything to do with Jesus. So she and her sister rigged a bag for the women. In the bottom, they put the Jesus video and the picture books. Then they covered them up with the pans and Tupperware in which the women had brought their meat loafs and cakes and potato salads.

One of the women picked up the bag. The weight of it surprised her. "I don't think this is all ours," she protested.

Amber and her sister assured her it was. "It's all yours," they promised.

Amber tells this story with some glee. She's gotten the food without having to pay for it with Jesus. Something for nothing. She's adept at playing the system.

I ignore my worm of disapproval and present my version of missionary meat loaf: a bag of mini Snicker bars and a slim, hardbound anthology of local poets from my own bookshelf. I'm not the first one to bring candy. On the bed, along with the TV remote and her cordless phone (complete with Caller ID), are a bag of jelly beans and carton of yellow marshmallow chicks. From time to time she pops one of the peepers. My mouth waters for a Snickers, but she doesn't open the bag.

She does open my book of poems, scans a few pages, and looks up at me in surprise. "These are much better than mine!" she protests.

I suggest, "Just read and enjoy them. Maybe you'll get some ideas for your own." My book disappears under her bed. I'm willing to bet she won't open it again.

On the TV, a darkly handsome man in a designer charcoal-gray silk shirt furrows his brow. He is a writer. He's just realized that the plot of his new novel has an ominous correspondence to real life. He steadies himself with a tanned hand on the edge of his desk.

Amber asks me if there is a pile of lumber outside. "Wayne says he's going to build a new front porch."

I say that I didn't notice any lumber on my way in. I go outside for a look and find a stack of pressure treated decking in the side yard. Paranoia at work? Or does Wayne have a habit of spending the money somewhere else?

As a defense against the TV, I have brought my needlepoint along. I show her the half-worked canvas, a Victorian-style rose. "Do you mind if I sew?" I ask.

She says, no, her mother used to do it.

We watch the soaps, and I sew, and during the commercial breaks, we talk about her mother's death.

Amber was nineteen at the time, unaware of what her

mother was going through. "At the end," Amber says, "she could only eat fruit."

Her mother didn't want to go back to the hospital and tried, unsuccessfully, to hide her pain. She asked Amber: "Which would you rather have: me in pain or me dead?"

"Oh, Amber!" I protest. "That's awful! She expected you to *choose?*"

She shrugs. She says her mother had a store of pills. She expertly rolls off a sequence of narcotic names. She thinks her mother had been saving them up—hence her pain.

"So you think she decided to end it."

"Yeah. We never told anyone. We didn't want any trouble with the insurance."

"Was this your mother's room?"

She nods, eyes on the TV. The interior of a police station. It's supposed to be a gritty scene, but our hero's two-day beard looks Euro-chic and all the cops are young and slim as models.

Again, Amber tells me how she had broken down her mother's door and demonstrates her mother's position on the bed.

"Is this the same bed?"

"No. We did the room over. But not right away." She's a bit defensive. "There was no point in us staying in that little room."

"You and Wayne had the boys' room?"

"Yeah." She pops another peeper.

I finish a little patch of creamy pink on my opulent rose and stare at the tangle of wool threads: mauve, salmon, crimson, rust. I think of my father's death. He died in a Connecticut hospital. I didn't make it home to Connecticut in time to be present, but the night before his funeral, he appeared in a dream. In the dream, I was sitting at his desk in his study, trying to figure out what tip to pay on one of his bills. In real life, my father's tipping habits were mortifying; he tipped according to 1920 standards, 10 percent tops. In the dream, I saw a six written in his handwriting at the top of the bill and my heart sank. *Six* percent? Hoping against hope, I asked him, "What do you want to tip?"

"The usual," he instructed.

"What's that?"

"Sixty percent," he said.

A violent shock of astonishment jolted me awake.

"Did you dream about your mother after she died?" I ask. It's a selfish question, something I want to know for me, not a "listening" response to something she's said.

The question turns her head from the TV screen. She stares at me. "Yes. I did."

I explain: "After my father died, I had a dream in which I knew he was dead, but at the same time he was alive and had changed. He did something completely out of character."

"Yes," she says. "That's exactly it. I knew she was dead but she was also alive."

But she does not elaborate.

At one point, I did ask if her father had abused her. She said no, he was "just completely selfish." He left about the time Amber was born. Amber was the youngest of three sisters. One sister was still in touch with him, but now "she's beginning to see what he's like." The other sister "lives somewhere in Pennsylvania." She doesn't know about Amber's cancer; Amber hasn't spoken to her in years. All Amber knows about her is that she is "real successful." She has a job with an electric company and "makes good money."

"Did you ever work outside the home?" I ask.

"Just at Kmart," she says. "It was only for a couple of months, then I got sick."

One of the cats comes in and gracefully leaps up into my

chair. He snuggles down in my lap, but he keeps shifting position and scratching himself so it's hard for me to sew. I bump him off.

"He's got fleas real bad," Amber informs me. "He's just been going crazy with them."

Now, as I write this, I'm itching under my T-shirt and wondering if I've brought home something more tangible than low-grade despair.

She forestalls any more of my questions by popping a pill. According to the list of medications she had written out, it was for "severe pain."

I feel a little shocked. "Are you in pain now?"

"Claire says I can take them to help me sleep."

I don't say anything, but I don't believe her. I suspect she is playing me against Claire, testing the loopholes in our system. She asks me if I've ever tried Ativan. I tell her I know nothing about it, that she needs to ask Claire, that I've worked with Claire before and I'm really impressed with her knowledge of pain control.

Amber mentions that Dr. Houck (her oncologist and the medical director of Blue Ridge Hospice) called. "I think he was surprised that I was still here." She pauses. "I guess maybe the kids are too. Wayne told them a couple months ago. They must be wondering why I'm not dead yet."

It was marginally better this time. I think she was disappointed to see me go. I only stayed two hours, but I'd had it. When I asked her if she would be okay, she said yes, I'll only be alone for three hours. So that made me feel guilty. On the other hand, her pill was kicking in and she was beginning to get fuzzy. I asked if she'd like me to rub her back or her feet, and she said no, with great certainty.

So I took her hand, gave it a little a squeeze, and said, "Enjoy your pill." And she gave me this big knowing smile. As if I were a fellow conspirator.

APRIL 6, MONDAY

Conversation with Milly, the new volunteer coordinator, about Amber's mother's history. Milly, who had just gone through an in-service on suicide, pounced with a label: suicide ideation. "But it's *my* idea, not Amber's," I objected. I don't feel I'm getting through. I worry that Milly's going to start pushing alarm buttons.

So I talked to Mare Rockwood. We agreed that it might not be a good idea to broach the subject of suicide directly. "We don't want to ideate for her," Mare said. We decided that Claire should approach the question of pain—of Amber's own pain as well as her mother's.

"How are you doing in there?" Mare asked.

I groaned. "It's pretty depressing. I had to leave early."

"Do you want off the case?"

The question took me by surprise. It had not occurred to me that I could pull out. The possibility is bracing: a breath of outside air. I find I don't want off. Bizarrely enough, I want to know how it's going to end.

I spend the weekend moving. I walk, practice tai chi, work out on Nautilus, strip and revarnish the wooden walls in our bathroom, hike up into the Shenandoah National Park with Andy. That Plexiglas cylinder has lifted. It's finally cooled off. And, going over the last visit with Amber, I see that in a small way, I have in fact, connected with her.

APRIL 8, WEDNESDAY

Monthly volunteer meeting. I present my case and a fellow volunteer exclaims in sympathy: "Soap operas are the penance of hospice volunteers!"

I tell the group that usually, when I leave a patient's house and get in my car, I take off my hospice ID pin before driving away; I literally "unpin" myself from the patient. With Amber, I admit, this ritual doesn't seem to be enough. I'm swamped by her.

Milly: "What Amber has created in her house is hers. It stays with her. When you leave the house, leave her life at the door."

"How?"

"When you go into the house, imagine leaving. The freedom is there for you."

Charlotte Stanton, Director of Nursing, suggests, "When you drive out, imagine leaving it all behind you in the woods."

I leave the meeting feeling hopeful, up for trying out my shiny new tools.

APRIL 9, THURSDAY

I drive out in a cool spring rain with new tires on my front wheels and find they've put down new gravel on the maze of roads. I get lost again. Everything looks different. The tangle of briars above the ditches has burst into green leaf, the tops of the trees are fuzzy: gold, pale green, bronze. Little half-opened umbrellas of mayapple make green patches on the floor of the woods. In the clearings under power lines, the redbud's spectacular, pink on wet black branches.

I bring another milk shake, prearranged by phone. (She nixed the burger. "They're always cold by the time they get here." I wonder who else brings her fast food.) So I know she's expecting me. But the front door is locked. I knock. No answer. There I am standing in the rain with my milk shake and my sewing and I think of Amber's mother dead behind her locked door. I wonder if Amber has "done it"—timed it for me. I bang on the door again. Still no answer.

Shit. Am I going to have to break in the way she broke into her dead mother's bedroom? Do I drive back out, find a phone, call her, call hospice if there's no answer, drive back in?

Then Amber opens up, apologizes for locking me out. She gives no explanation. She is not using her walker. She's quick and light on her feet. She darts back to her bedroom, settles down on the bed. I see she has painted her toenails purple-black. She asks me to nuke a Hot♦Pocket for her lunch. This comestible turns out to be something that looks like a cross between a turnover and a burrito. She has a freezer full of them in two flavors: beef and chicken. The packaging is elaborate and the directions are mysterious: "Insert Pocket into crisper sleeve. . . ." Crisper sleeve? I feel as if I've landed in a foreign country. I run back and forth between kitchen and bedroom with questions. My ignorance entertains her.

I'm trying to figure out her microwave when there's a knock at the door. It's a young woman from the church delivering a load of food: meat loaf, gravy, potatoes, ham sandwiches, cake.

I decide she's the reason for the locked door. So I play guardian at the gate and lie. "Amber's dozing," I tell her. I add, "I don't think she's up for a visit right now."

The girl is a bit taken aback. "Oh. I was just dropping this off," she tells me. "I've got all the kids out in my car. Just tell her I love her." She's so bright and bouncy and cheerful that I feel sorry for her. I exclaim over her food, praise her generosity.

After she leaves, Amber, whom I'm certain has been eavesdropping, appears in the kitchen to inspect the haul. "She's just using me for her own needs," she says.

I defend the girl, then realize that Amber has shut down. "Well, you know the situation better than I do," I say.

She re-engages. "I just think it's kind of hypocritical for them to pay all this attention to me."

We watch the soaps, I sew, and during commercial breaks for instant snack foods and over-the-counter drugs (twin pillars of our culture?), I ask her a question and we talk a bit. I find the ads much more interesting than the soaps and have to concentrate on not getting sucked into them—otherwise we'd have no conversation at all.

We talk about her medication (Claire has prescribed a new tranquilizer for her and she thinks maybe it's helping) and about the book of poems I gave her. She says she's read several. I doubt it and don't quiz her on which ones. Read or unread, my gift of other people's poems seems to have killed any hope for her own.

We also talk about her kids: JJ and Brett, five and seven. She worries what will become of them but feels powerless to do much of anything for them. She worries that Wayne is abusing the generosity of the friends and neighbors who pick them up after school; Wayne stays at work till 6:30 or 7:00 P.M., she says.

The kids are seeing a counselor at school—against Amber's wishes. She had told the counselor no, she didn't want the kids to be singled out. I think she wants their life to be as normal as possible. She wants to spare them what's coming and let them deal with it when she's gone.

If nothing else, Amber makes me realize how middle-class my mind-set is: in my comfortable world, library books are to be returned and children are to be prepared for the worst.

The counselor, apparently, shares my sensibility—at least in the matter of children. She ignored Amber's wishes (perhaps Amber had not expressed them forcefully enough) and pulled the boys out of class for a therapy session. They came home with some sort of craft, and seemed to like the counselor, so Amber didn't complain. "But it makes me angry," she says—without discernable emotion.

I tell her I'd be angry too. I tell her that, according to hospice philosophy, she's the one to call the shots. "We're here to support your decisions about what's best for your kids," I assure her. *Nonetheless*, I can't resist sneaking in a suggestion about what I think would be best for her kids. I tell her that I think it would be a good idea if she met Mare Rockwood, just so she knew who she was, and that perhaps Mare could help Wayne with plans for the boys' care.

She turns back to the TV without responding. But during the next commercial, she says she thinks she could meet Mare if I was there. I feel a small flood of relief. I tell her I'll bring Mare along with me next week, that she will have her own car, and will only stay for a short while.

She offers me a chocolate—a box of elegantly wrapped bonbons—gold foil, black ruffled paper, "Prodotto dalla Ferrera." Expensive-looking. I take one. It's perfectly delicious: milky, silky chocolate with a hazelnut inside. I bravely decline a second one—which makes her worry that I hadn't really liked the first. "They are a little rich," she apologizes. I reassure her that they are the most delicious chocolates I'd ever eaten and that if she wasn't careful, I'd gobble them all up. Turns out these are the chocolates she had been looking for on my first visit, the ones she thought Wayne had thrown out. Her sister had found them under the *other* side of the bed.

She still voices suspicions about Wayne: "I wonder what he's done with my Blazer—where he's put it. He said he sold it, said he got four thousand for it—not that I'd mind if he did. I won't be using it." But she doubts that he'd managed to get that much. "We're over two thousand in debt," she tells me.

I make us tea. She seems softer, a bit more open. Perhaps it's the new tranquilizer. Perhaps it's the beginning of trust. Perhaps it won't last. But she lets me hug her when I leave—a nice long hug. She straightens her turban and shyly thanks me for coming. I realize that she doesn't look so strange anymore and that her voice is quite lovely.

I leave feeling pretty good. I'm halfway out of the hollow before I remember my resolve to make my leaving a conscious separation. I decide that it doesn't matter that I'm feeling good this time, I still need a division between my life and hers. I'd forgotten to wear my pin in the house, so I couldn't take it off, but when I hit hardtop, I imagine leaving the whole three hours—from Hot♦Pocket to hug—in the woods behind me.

EDNA

Footfalls echo in the memory
Down the passage which we did not take
Towards the door we never opened
Into the rose-garden.

—T. S. Eliot, *Four Quartets*, Burnt Norton, 1

WHEN I stood on Amber's deck and banged on her locked door in
the rain, it was not only the prospect of suicide that clutched at
my heart. It was a chill blast from the past. The prospect of being
shut out raised the specter of Edna.

Edna is wreathed in smoke. She is fifty-nine and dying of lung
cancer but still pulling furiously on her Virginia Slims. Her face is
seamed and leathery as an old turtle's and her voice is husky and
ironic, but she has the vulnerable eyes of a child who has been
frightened awake in the night. She locked me out twice: at the
beginning; and then four months later, after what I mistakenly
thought was her end.

Her husband had requested a volunteer to sit with her on the
nights his church group met but when I called to introduce

myself to set up an initial meeting, Edna brushed me off. "I don't need a volunteer," she snapped.

"That's okay," I said, keeping my voice bright. "I'll check back with you next week." I called twice more, and each time she refused. Finally, in exasperation I pushed. "I'm part of the package," I said. "You should at least meet me, in case you need me later on."

Silence. Then, in a small, timid voice she agreed to see me. The threat of "later on" had worked. I felt like a bully.

She lived in an older subdivision of small boxy houses built in the 1950s. I rang her doorbell at the appointed time, a January afternoon. The maples out on the street had been brutally topped by the power company; they stood like stiff-bristled brushes against the cold gray sky. I waited on the doorstep, straining for sounds of footsteps on the other side of the door but the house was ominously still. With a stab of panic, I wondered if I had mistaken the day. Or had she fallen? Was she lying on the floor unable to answer the door? Had she died?

I rang again. I tried knocking. I waited and rang and knocked and gave up. I walked back to my car, got inside, slipped my key in the ignition—then pulled it out. I decided to try one more time.

This time, the door opened a crack. I felt a flood of relief. I saw a slight woman in a bathrobe peering at me through the glass of the storm door. "Hello," I said. "I'm Christine from hospice. Were you asleep? I hope I didn't wake you."

She turned and fled back into the house. I stood on the doorstep, wondering what to do now. I rapped lightly on the storm door. No response. I waited some more. I was about to leave when she reappeared. Without a word, she unlatched the door for me. Ducking her head as if I were wielding a large club, she scurried off and I followed into the living room where she dove into a little heap of blankets on the floor in front of the TV

and pulled an afghan over her head. The afghan was made of crocheted brown and orange squares and clashed rudely with the
room's pale lilac decor.

I knelt down on the pastel carpet, keeping my distance, and
sat back on my heels, my purse still hanging from my shoulder,
my coat still buttoned. I saw that the pile of blankets was trembling. She peeked out at me with the frightened eyes of a cor-
nered animal.

Nonchalantly, I let my eyes go to the TV. I pretended to be
interested in *One Life to Live*. After several minutes my knees
began to protest and I asked, "Would you like me to leave?"

"No, that's okay," she said. She emerged shakily from her
nest, lit up a Virginia Slim and glommed onto the TV. At the
next commercial, she stubbed out her cigarette and moved into
her bedroom. She lay down on the bed and asked me to hook her
up to her oxygen canister. She began to relax a little. She told me
she had just come home from the hospital and was unable to eat
anything or even swallow liquids. She was angry that she had not
been allowed to smoke in the hospital—"discrimination," she
called it.

She told me that she'd had a bad reaction to morphine: she
had attacked the doctor, tried to claw his eyes out, had managed
to land a kick in his ribs before they strapped her down. She told
the story with pride. There was also pride in her voice when she
declared, "I've accepted my death."

Acceptance notwithstanding, by my next visit, it looked as if
she had decided to live. She had started eating and drinking
again, was even enjoying an unaccustomed glass of sweet wine
before meals. I asked her if she would like to make a tape of her
memories for her son—her only child (now twenty-something)
from a previous marriage. She was enthusiastic about the project
and in between visits, would fill index cards and the backs of

envelopes with notes for our sessions with my tape recorder. Her recall of her son's childhood was amazing. In painstaking detail, she recorded what he ate, what scrapes he got into, which friends he played with, what grades he got from which teacher. It was as if she had unlocked a retrospective daily diary. I found the taping tedious, in the way that listening, hour after hour, to a mother praising her child is tedious, but I liked watching her face as she told her stories. Her eyes sparkled, her leathery face crinkled with pleasure.

Despite the intimacy of the taping, I did not feel any special connection to Edna; the chemistry that I had felt with Bivie Peterson simply was not there, but I felt pleased that she had come to trust me and it was very satisfying to imagine her son receiving the gift of her tape.

One afternoon, as Edna talked into my tape recorder, I felt a shift, a kind of subtle radiance in the room. I became aware of the ticking of the antique clock on the mantel. It was a reminder that Edna's time was running out, yet I had a sense of being outside of time—or entirely in it. Every molecule in the room simply *was*.

This had happened to me before with other patients. Some with whom I felt a "connection," others with whom I never exchanged a word, who were comatose. The shift in Edna's lilac living room seemed entirely arbitrary, a mysterious accident of the job. In my journal, I wrote: "Hard to know what this is, or describe it—but when it happens, it's unmistakable—and it informs my days with a kind of luminescence."

I was reminded of the long-ago interview I'd done with hospice volunteers for *Virginia Country* magazine. Mary Jane Lee, face aglow, had marveled, "What's so wonderful about sitting with an old man listening to him talk about his chickens?" Was she talking about this kind of mystical perk? Whatever the answer, it led her to become a hospice nurse.

After one February visit to Edna, I had a dream. I was at the house on Long Island Sound of a gentle, elegant older cousin whom I called Aunt Dora and who had died some years previously. In my dream, it was late afternoon in winter but the lawn looked as green as summer and the sinking sun cast a golden light on the waters beyond the seawall. It was dead calm. I was shocked to see that her house was no longer there, only an outline of foundation stones in the rich green grass. Then I saw Aunt Dora in a bright red wool coat, tailored princess-style. She was walking down the lawn and looked as beautiful as ever, except her skin looked as if she were already dead. I realized she had cancer. She was accompanied by her husband and her son. Both men hovered protectively and wore formal dark business suits, the sort one might expect to see at a funeral. They did not want me to acknowledge her cancer in any way.

So I said to her, "Do you remember your beautiful garden?" The question made the men angry: "What's gone is gone," they objected. I felt as if I was barging in, disturbing a precarious balance.

However, Aunt Dora's face lit up and together we began remembering the garden with its pergola and its little fountain and astonishingly, the house resurrected itself around us. We were back in her living room with its view of the sound and its piano and a piece of needlepoint she remembered working on as a child. It was a joyous, poetic moment, but her husband—my Uncle Marshie—put a stop to it. "You've got a good bag of tricks," he scolded, "but you can't fool me."

I woke up stunned. Upon reflection, I decided that my unconscious had twisted my dear, sweet Uncle Marshie into a representation of my disbelieving rational self. So I pushed him out of the way and focused on the figure of Aunt Dora. I associated my magical moment in Aunt Dora's reconstructed living room with the blissful luminescence I'd experienced in Edna's living room. But Aunt Dora's red coat puzzled me. What did that mean? The red was insistent, as deep and vibrant as the color of blood.

In my journal, I copied out a passage from Clarissa Pinkola Estes's *Women Who Run with the Wolves*: "There is throughout the world a figure known as the red mother. She is not as well known as the black mother or madonna, but she is the watcher of 'things coming through.' She is especially propitiated by those about to give birth, for whosoever leaves this world or comes into this world has to pass through her red river."

I had never heard of a red mother before. But it struck me that like Estes' red goddess, the Aunt Dora of my dream was a transitional figure: dying but not dead. She was *en passant*, wearing a coat, not a dress. Like my patient Edna, she was remembering her past as she waited for her death. Like Edna, she was neither here nor there.

Time has enlarged my perspective: now I remember that in real life, my Aunt Dora was a volunteer at our local hospital, and that she was the one who enabled me, at age fourteen, to work as a candy striper delivering flowers to patients' bedsides. She was the one who initiated me into the pleasures of halos. (Far easier to wear in the hospital than at home!)

Also, instead of dismissing Uncle Marshie's dark role in the dream, I now can bear to look closer. Through the zoom lens of hindsight, he seems to point to Edna's husband, Ray. Now, in fact, the dream seems an amazingly accurate warning.

Ray worked for the sheriff's department in another county. He was a pudgy man, with an agreeable round face, who was protective of Edna. Although she was ambulatory and could pretty much fend for herself, he did not want her to be alone during the day, so he hired a daytime caregiver for her, a young single mother named Jeanette who cleaned and cooked and ran errands. Edna and Jeanette smoked together and watched the afternoon soaps together. If I arrived during a favorite, they could barely tear themselves away to talk to me.

Edna had also bonded with Lee, the hospice nurse, who shared Edna's taste for biting sarcasm. Jeanette's eyes would widen as Edna and Lee exchanged wisecracks. "Lee really cuts up with Edna," she would marvel to me.

"Hmm," I would say with a noncommittal smile. But the blade-work made me uneasy. What was not aimed at men in general was aimed at Ray. He seemed a nice enough man. He usually came home from work about the time I was ready to leave, so our conversations were in passing. Once he expressed his anger that Edna refused to give up her cigarettes, refused to try for healing, refused to try for a miracle. I felt sorry for what he was going through.

Still, on the surface, everything appeared to be moving smoothly. Then suddenly we were all inside a soap opera of our own. On the phone and out of Edna's hearing, Jeanette complained to me that Ray was hitting on her. She was afraid she would lose her job if Edna found out. Edna, it seemed, clung to Ray with a fierce jealousy. She could not bear to think of him with another woman. Her jealousy was aggravated by calls to the house from Ray's ex-wife who seemed to be circling overhead like a raptor ready to plunge.

Ray, at least in front of me, dismissed his ex-wife's advances with self-deprecating jokes. "She just wants to recycle her garbage," he would declare, but clearly her attentions had perked him up. Ray had been feeling jealous himself—of Edna's relationship with her son. According to Jeanette, he was angry that Edna spent her days boxing up things for her son. "The only reason he comes to visit you," he would tell Edna, "is to make sure your money goes to him instead of me." Jeanette confided that Ray had a mean temper and she was frightened for Edna.

This is only the barest of plot outlines. The more I heard, the more it seemed that our soap had been scripted by the blackest of black humorists. Edna's past had its unresolved, violent losses, but there were also bizzare, macabre twists that captured the novelist in me. I was swept along into the powerful current of Edna's dying. If I was fascinated by the dark shapes under the surface, it never occurred to me that I could get hurt. I was too busy trying to navigate around the boulders above water.

I gave Jeanette a private pep talk on fending off Ray. She looked skeptical.

With Ray, I decided to try the magic of active listening. I thought perhaps if he could "vent" his feelings a bit, it might defuse the mounting level of tension in the house. It didn't work. Whenever I keyed into the emotional "subtext" of his stated concerns, whenever I said something like "That must be pretty worrisome for you," his face would darken and close and he would snap, "I'm all right."

Time for a pro, I thought. I asked our social worker Stefani Cochrane to contact Ray. She talked to him on the phone. "I thought we were having a pretty good talk," she reported back to me. "Then he blew up and told me that if I called again, he'd pull Edna out of hospice."

Now when Ray came home from work, Edna's shoulders would hunch up under her velour bathrobe. Her mouth would tighten like a trip wire and the light would go out of her eyes.

I asked her if Ray was abusive to her.

"Verbally," she said.

"If you didn't have cancer, would you get out of the marriage?" I asked.

"You bet," she said, exhaling a cloud of smoke. "He changed after we got married. One minute he could be sweet as you please, the next—" She broke off with shrug and took another pull on her cigarette.

I missed several visits on account of snowstorms and the next time I went, Edna's condition was much changed, as the hospice euphemism goes. Lee, the nurse, and Jeanette, the paid caregiver, were both there. Lee told me that Edna was sleeping most of the time and had been talking to her old dog who was long since dead. The three of us sat with Edna in her bedroom for a while and when she dozed off, we moved into the kitchen where we sat around the table drinking coffee.

Jeannette worried that Ray was still sniping at Edna. "Then when he's nice to her, she melts," Jeanette complained.

"He's all she has," I offered.

"She's got her son," Lee said drily. She raised a lewdly appreciative eyebrow. "He's a dish."

We laughed.

"Ray's not all bad," I insisted, sticking up for the man.

They looked at me as if I were nuts.

"He has sexual fantasies about you," Jeanette said bluntly.

"*Me?*"

"He says—"

"Don't tell me!" I cut her off in alarm. *Ray was unloading his sexual fantasies on Jeanette?*

"He talks about you too," she informed Lee.

Lee let out a resigned sigh. She confided that as a hospice nurse, she found sexual issues the hardest to deal with. "I have one patient whose husband keeps telling me that he hasn't had sex in two years."

"So what do you tell him?" I wonder.

Lee shrugged. "I say, 'Well, there are other outlets . . . ' "

"I can't imagine telling Ray it's okay to masturbate!" I exclaimed, my mind thoroughly boggled.

Jeanette snorted in disgust. "He worries about being too fat, then he gobbles up an entire macaroni and cheese casserole."

"He's worried he's too fat to attract a new woman," Lee decided.

"He should be," Jeannette said acidly.

But I couldn't brush off the matter of Ray's fantasies. I remembered that he had read one of my mysteries. After complimenting me on it, he had given me a sly look, as if he knew my secret. "Maybe he's got me confused with my protagonist," I said.

"Your what?" asked Jeanette.

"The heroine in my book. She has the hots for this law-enforcement guy."

Lee, who had borrowed the book from another nurse, said, "You mean she's not you? There's no little girl?" (My sleuth had a daughter who died of leukemia at age four.)

"I never had a child who died," I told Lee. "I've never been divorced. I have two grown sons and have been happily married to the same man for over twenty-five years."

Lee looked disappointed. She stood up to go. "Someone should call Edna's son," she instructed. "It could be anytime."

Moments after Lee left, Edna came into the kitchen and sat with Jeanette and me, as if she couldn't bear to miss the party. Guiltily, I wondered if she'd heard me talking about Ray masturbating. Then Ray came home and Jeanette left.

Since the last time I had seen him, he had gained at least twenty pounds. The buttons on his tan uniform shirt pulled at his chest and his belly had gotten so big that his fly would not zip all the way up. He lumbered nervously around the kitchen.

"Now sit down," Edna bossed him. He sat down at the table with us. I was relieved; his gaping fly was out of sight. Edna told him he should call her son. He nodded meekly. "Your dinner's in the microwave," she informed him.

"I'm eating for two," he said guiltily to me. To Edna, he said, "I wish I could eat for you." His voice was tender, full of longing.

I stood up to leave. Edna turned up her face like a child saying good night. I kissed her gently on the forehead and wondered if I would see her again.

"Let me talk to you a minute," I said to Ray. He stepped out the back door with me. We stood on the stoop in the cold. I told him that Lee felt Edna was getting close. He marveled at her lack of pain and admitted he was still angry about her Virginia Slims. "She's up to two packs a day."

I said something about it being hard to let someone you love go. I asked if he felt able to say good-bye to her. I explained that saying good-bye could be a kind of "giving permission," that it seemed to make it easier for the dying person to let go.

To my disconcertment, he swaggered a little and boasted that he'd been taught five ways to kill a man.

Surely not sheriff's department training. "In the military?"

"Yes," he said.

Driving home, I puzzled over his strange boast. Could it be true? Ray as a commando was a reach. Had he been trying to impress me with his familiarity with death? Was he telling me that he was not afraid to see his wife die?

I thought about the kitchen-table chat and I thought about Edna, how her eyes had shone when I kissed her forehead. I felt that I had been too talky. I resolved to come back the next day and sit quietly with her instead of gabbing in the kitchen. If she didn't die in the night.

Early the next morning Lee called to say that Edna had made it through the night and, *mirabile dictu*, was scarfing down breakfast. She was bright-eyed and bushy-tailed, planning to go out for lunch with a friend and out for dinner with Ray.

I wondered if the tenderness Ray had shown her had bounced her back.

Four days later, I called the house. Jeanette told me Edna was asleep. I told her to tell Edna I'd come by that afternoon at one o'clock—my usual day, usual time. Fine, she said.

There were two cars in the driveway and one parked out front on the street. I parked behind it and walked around the house to the back door, which was left open when they were home. As usual, I knocked and turned the doorknob to go in. The door was locked. The little panes of glass set in the door had been curtained off and the shades were down on all the windows. I felt a shock, then a rush of shame. I was shut out. I knocked, rang the doorbell three, four times. I felt sure they were inside and wondered why they weren't answering the door. Had she died? Was she dying and they didn't want me or anyone else there? I walked around to the front door and rang the bell. I felt as if the entire neighborhood was watching me through their windows. Still no answer. Was the bell working? Had Edna been taken to the hospital? Or had she just decided to go somewhere at the last minute? It was a pretty spring day. Had she gone for a drive? But why all the cars? I tried the back door one more time, then left a note saying I would call later in the week. I felt annoyed that Edna had not had the courtesy to let me know she was going out.

Later that afternoon, Rhonda Headley, the volunteer coordinator, reached me at home to say that Edna didn't want me in the house anymore. She had told Lee that I'd been making sexual advances to Ray. I was off the case.

I felt as if I'd been beaten up. I felt betrayed and humiliated. Like any victim, over and over I tried to figure out what I had done wrong. Rhonda and the hospice staff were extremely supportive.

Collectively, they spent hours on the phone with me. I wondered cynically if my board of director's hat had primed the flow of their kindness. Stefani, the social worker whom Ray had blasted, called to commiserate. Lee called and suggested that Edna had been eavesdropping in the hall as we talked in the kitchen.

But there was no way to sort it out. Perhaps Edna had heard me sticking up for Ray and, when I asked him to step outside, suspected the worst.

Perhaps Jeanette had set me up to protect herself.

Or perhaps Ray, during a fight, had taunted Edna with sexual boasts about me.

I sifted two lessons out of the wreckage: 1. Never to talk to a female patient's husband out of her presence; 2. Never talk *about* the husband out of her presence.

I sent Edna the last tape we had been working on and enclosed a good-bye note wishing her "peace of mind and heart."

In my journal, I copied a prayer written by Rabindranath Tagore:

> *Let me not pray to be sheltered from dangers but to be fearless*
> *   in facing them.*
> *Let me not beg for the stilling of my pain but for the heart to*
> *   conquer it.*
> *Let me not look for allies in life's battlefield but to my own*
> *   strength.*
> *Let me not crave in anxious fear to be saved but hope for the*
> *   patience to win my freedom.*
> *Grant that I may not be a coward, feeling your mercy in my*
> *   success alone; but let me find the grasp of your hand in my*
> *   failure.*

Gradually I began to regard my failure as naïveté. I had assumed that because my intentions were good, sweetness and light would follow and we would all be transformed and healed. Despite beat-you-over-the-head clues, I had ignored the darker side of Edna's death: her animal-like fear on my first visit; the bizarre *noire* tidbits from her past; Ray's panicky sexuality.

It dawned on me that Edna's dying was an empowerment. For the first time in her eight-year marriage to Ray—maybe for the first time in her life—she had leverage. Death gave her a way to get back at Ray for wounds inflicted. She had the pleasure of lighting up a cigarette and watching him cringe, of closing her eyes and having him spring to her side. Her weakness made him contrite.

I began to see the end of life as a time of power, power that can be used for better or worse. I began to see that while dying can be a time for the fullness and the freedoms of love, it can also be a time for payback, for jerking the strings of one's nearest if not dearest.

Gradually I saw that my wound was not so much a clawed heart as a punctured ego: Edna had rejected me. I had lavished my time on her for four months. I had given her tapes for her son, I had been kind to her husband, I had been supportive of her caregiver. And she had slammed the door in my face.

After a week of a flu-like malaise, a sense of absurdity gave me a healthy nudge. In all my agonizing over the case, I'd overlooked a very basic fact: *It was not me who was dying!*

I don't know how or when Edna died. I remember that Rhonda called to tell me that she had died, and I have the feeling it was some months after I got kicked out, but I didn't bother to write it down. The last thing I wrote in my journal about Edna was: "I think of her as an angry she-bear hiding under an afghan of crocheted granny squares. I got too close and got scratched. It may be important to recognize the bear in people who are dying."

Mare and I arrive in separate cars. Over the weekend, Wayne replaced the sagging landing outside the front door with a new deck built from the pile of treated lumber in the side yard. The steps leading up to it have been spray-painted silver—the kids' work, it looks like. Bees swarm under the eaves. It's warm and overcast.

Mare, small and dark and wiry, is wearing her long hair loose and a long flouncy skirt. She is dressed like a schoolgirl in *Little House on the Prairie,* but her jaw is set as if she has taken three deep breaths before getting out of her Blazer. She strides up the silver steps in her long skirt and I remember that she is an athlete—a serious horsewoman.

I bring another milk shake. Amber, mindful perhaps of my incompetence with last week's Hot♦Pocket, asks for Ramen noodles. She's left a packet out on the kitchen counter for me, along with a bowl. This I can do. I boil water while Mare visits with Amber. She's not wearing her turban. Bald and sitting cross-legged on the bed, her smooth skin and double chins suggest a Chinese Buddha. The unsmiling variety. But she seems relaxed and more open, more willing to talk about Wayne, about her concerns for the kids. She gives us a note from Claire expressing "concern" that no arrangements have been made for the boys' care for the coming summer. Reading between the lines, I sense Claire's irritation and frustration.

Amber tells us that she's looking for day care, but she isn't sure she wants or can afford a sitter in the house.

After Mare leaves, I remake Amber's bed for her. She complains about dry skin and lets me rub her arms and legs with lotion—cocoa butter, it says on the label. It's the first time she's let me do this for her. She smells like the beach.

We settle into the soaps. She talks a bit more about the kids: how Wayne's too easy on them, easier than her, but she doesn't want to always be the heavy, she doesn't want them to remember her as always "hollering at them all the time." Bivie, I remember, had the same concern.

The ceiling fan over her bed is on and the sliding door to a deck outside her room is open. There's no screen. Bees keep floating in and I keep shooing them out. In the woods at the edge of the yard, birds are raising an extraordinary racket—loud enough to distract Amber from her soaps. It sounds as if all their nests are being attacked at once. An entire orchestra of twittering and tweeting. I step outside onto the deck, but see nothing to explain the sustained crescendo, only a strong wind out of the west and the smell of rain. The air is clean and full of expectation.

I go back inside and ask her about the bird in her attic. She hops out of bed and goes into the boys' bedroom and snatches up one of JJ's plastic dinosaurs: she moves its back legs and it emits a throaty moan. I shut my eyes. It sounds as if a pigeon is in the room. The solution to the mystery pleases her; Wayne was right after all.

APRIL 23, THURSDAY

This time I bring a small bottle of sesame oil. The nurses recommend it for dry skin; I've added a dollop of lavender oil to make it less kitcheny-smelling. I also bring three Xeroxed copies of poems by Henry Taylor. Monday night, he read at the college and I was caught up by his passion, his humor, his almost priestly devotion to his Muse. Oil for the body, poetry for the soul. My offerings please me.

I drive out anticipating a good visit and find her dull and sleepy. She asks for a repeat with the Ramen, plus half a chicken sandwich. "Lots of mayo," she orders. In the fridge I find a gallon jar of mayonnaise and a perfectly roasted chicken. Someone has sliced off just enough breast meat for half a sandwich. I gob the mayo on a slice of "air" bread, slide it all the way out to the crusts. I look at it. *She couldn't like that much.* I scrape a little off. But when she eats it, I see she is swallowing with some effort. "Did I make it too dry for you?" I ask. "Let me put some more mayonnaise on it. It's no trouble."

"It's fine," she lies politely.

"Are you sure? Sandwiches are a very personal thing," I assure her. "My husband won't trust me to make his."

"It's fine," she insists.

Her bedroom seems lighter, airier. I realize that her curio cabinet and its collection of china cats, plastic horses, and Beanie Babies is gone; she tells me that her friend Debby had moved it for her into the living room. The living room is so dark, I'd missed it on the way through.

In the process of cleaning and sorting they had found frames for some of Amber's loose snapshots. I zero in on a three-by-five of her and Wayne. It looks as if it were taken at a party. He is shirtless, handsome, hefty on the way to fat. She is vamping for the camera. Her long red fingernails dig into his bare chest like a tiger's claws. Her hair falls to her shoulders in a lustrous tangle of chestnut curls. She looks young and sexy and wild.

She says sorting through her pictures made her eyes "swim." "It made me dizzy. I saw specks."

"Maybe it's the tumor," I offer.

"Yes." My concern seems to perk her up.

After lunch we watch the soaps. She clues me in. "There's been another murder."

"Are there usually murders on the soaps?" I ask.

"I guess so."

I tell her I watch *NYPD Blue* and *Homicide: Life on the Streets.*

"Oh, I don't like that kind of show at all!"

So I suppose she will not like my offering of Taylor's "Landscape with Tractor," the story of a man mowing hay and discovering the body of a "well-dressed black woman" with "two bullet holes in her breast." Bad pick. I chose it because it was accessible and because it was about life and death and because it gave me a thrilling little prickle of recognition.

The tractor driver demands:

*. . . And I ask you
again, how would it be? To go on with your life, putting gas
in the tractor, keeping down the thistles*

*and seeing, each time you pass that spot,
the form in the grass . . .*

and to know she will stay in that field till you die?

So much for my new fantasy: to nourish Amber's soul with something more real than the noise of soaps; to give her "a taste of the movement of inner life" as poet Robert Hass puts it. Well, I'm probably safe: chances are she won't read it.

She tells me that Wayne wants her to do more, to fold laundry, to relieve him of some of the burden. For her part, she wants him to get used to running the house without her. I have the sense that she is testing him, that she could do more if she wanted. As it is, she cleans up after breakfast, washes the dishes, wipes the counters. The kitchen is always pristine when I come. But she wants to see him managing it all on his own. She doesn't quite trust him, but she wants to.

She says he told her he wasn't going to marry again. When I told her that Greg Peterson had not remarried, she seemed pleased. She thinks Wayne would not go out and find someone new. "He's too shy. If he remarries," she speculates, "it'll be someone he already knows." She has reviewed all the possible candidates and takes some satisfaction in the fact that none are available.

She falls asleep.

She is snoring, the TV is blaring, and I'm thinking, *What the hell am I doing here?* Then I think, *Just be here.* I breathe into my golden ball of light, and try to keep track of the story so I can tell her if she wakes up and asks. I watch a beating: a furiously jealous white girl straddles her best friend black girl on a white sofa and whacks her about the head and shoulders with a white cordless phone. I watch betrayals, lies, and sacrifices. I wonder about the changed room. I remember that Bivie, just before the end, had cleaned out her room with the help of her sisters. I wonder if Amber's sleeping is a "change"—a sign that she is nearing death. Or is it simply that she is she comfortable enough with me to doze off?

At 2:30 P.M. I wake her and tell I have to go.

"Already?" she says.

I tell her about the beating she'd slept through, then lean over the bed and give her a kiss.

APRIL 24, FRIDAY

Itching again under my clothes. Maybe I should spray myself with
Off! the next time.

APRIL 30, THURSDAY

Short visit. Andy recovering at home from his shoulder surgery
and I didn't want to leave him alone for too long. At issue: how
much Amber can do.

She asks me to get her a sandwich and a cup of tea for lunch.
This time she's taking no chances. I find the sandwich premade
in the fridge and the kettle on low. While I'm in the kitchen, she
pops in and takes a bag of chips down from the top of the fridge
and hands them to me. She darts back into her bedroom. I gar-
nish her sandwich with chips and carry the plate in to her. As she
eats, she complains about Wayne: he wants her to do more
around the house.

Claire is worried about the summer. Neither Amber nor
Wayne have made any move toward finding child care. Claire is
afraid that the everyday stress of caring for two boys will kick
Amber out of "remission." (Claire's use of the term is a surprise to
me. In this case it seems to mean a plateau, a stay in decline—not
a return to health.) So Claire has been pushing Amber to make
summer arrangements for the kids.

Amber, however, is focused on the immediate problem of
their after-school care. She asks Claire if hospice will provide
someone (as in me) to pick up the kids at school and watch them
till Wayne gets home. Claire tells her no. "We are not baby-
sitters," she scolds.

"I wanted to warn you," she tells me on the phone before this week's visit. Amber exasperates her. Apparently Amber will not let the aides help her with her bath. Like me, they mostly watch TV with her. Yesterday one of them was reassigned.

Now Amber is afraid we're going to drop her from the program. I explain that our census has hit an all time high and that we have patients who are completely bedridden and whose spouses are too old and frail to lift and turn and bathe them. "We just don't have enough aides to go around," I say.

With uncanny timing, Mare Rockwood calls in the middle of this discussion. She talks to Amber, then Amber passes the phone to me. Mare instructs me to reassure Amber that she is "an appropriate candidate for hospice." The soaps are blaring, Amber is talking to me in one ear, Mare in the other, and I'm trying to hear how what I'm saying to Mare sounds to Amber.

Mare says she thinks Amber might be having "some confusion." Mare tells me she's researched local summer day-care programs and says she'll send Amber the information and applications.

After I hang up, I tell Amber that I'll be glad to help her with the forms.

"I'm not sure I can fill them out," she admits.

I also tell her that I would like to come out one evening to meet Wayne and her boys.

"What for?"

"Just to meet them."

We look at each other.

"Amber," I say firmly. "I'm here for you. I'm not going to do anything behind your back. I just would like to meet your family. It might make things easier for them later on."

Amber is so acutely perceptive that I have a hard time thinking of her as "confused." On the other hand, she is convinced that on a previous visit, we'd had a long conversation on the meaning of "phat."

"*Fat?*" I wonder.

She spells it out for me. It's an acronym: Phenomenally Hot And Terrific—something like that. We had not talked about it before. She insists we had. "Maybe I forgot," I say.

I call Claire at home. "Amber thinks you're angry at her," I tell her.

"I am!" Claire admits with a laugh. "I'm really annoyed with her. I feel she's manipulating us."

"The tool of the powerless."

"What?"

"Manipulation."

"Christine, I'll try to patch it up with her, smooth things over, but I don't have time to play games with her. Six of my patients are actively dying. From now on, she's up to you."

Claire's handwashing is a surprise. I know that it is an emotional handwashing, that she will continue to visit Amber. Nonetheless, Claire is the team leader. I am discomforted by her "abdication" and at the same time flattered by her confidence in me. I try to imagine what it must be like to bounce back and forth between six deathbeds. My mind boggles.

We talk about the difficulty of the case: Amber's lack of affect, her distorted physical appearance, her sly maneuverings.

The big question: what is real? We see her disease, and the prospect of her death, but not the context of her life. What is a symptom of brain cancer and what is a by-product of her life? Her statements to us float in a vacuum. Is she confused and paranoid? Or are we? Is there any difference between my own greed for life and Amber's?

MAY 6, WEDNESDAY

As prearranged on the phone with Amber, I drive out early in the afternoon to meet Wayne—and the kids, as it turns out. They are home on an early school dismissal. I climb the silver steps, knock on the screen door, yoohoo and walk into the darkness inside. I see one of the kids at the dining-room table with his homework. It's JJ, the younger one. Wayne is standing over him, helping him. They look up. Wayne is shirtless and unshaven. A pale belly hangs over his belt. I introduce myself and he nods. His shyness is palpable.

I visit with Amber in her bedroom for a few minutes, then go into the kids' room to say hello to Brett. There's a TV on the dresser and he's playing a video game on it. He's sitting on the floor working the controls. I ask him the name of the game and he mumbles something I can't understand. Then Amber, who must have been listening in the hallway, appears and rescues us both. "This is my friend," she says to him. She is gracious, smiling, warm—a hostess making introductions.

Amber and I move outside to the new deck. She winces in the sunlight. "Do you want to go back in?" I ask.

"No."

I move her chair into a strip of shade. Wayne comes out and sits down with us. The dog lies at his feet, happily flapping his tail on the new decking. JJ, not wanting to miss anything, plays with the maple leaf seed pods littering the deck. I make conversation with Wayne about his building the deck. I ask how long they've been married. Seventeen years, he says.

It's a pretty day. The leaves on the trees are large and green but still floppy. After a week of rain, you almost hear the grass growing. The boys have summer buzz cuts. Their shorn heads look vulnerable: along the hairline at back, behind the ears, the newly exposed skin is milky white. I want to reach out and feel JJ's bristles under the curve of my palm.

He is playing close to the edge of the deck and Amber frets at him to get back. He ignores her.

I tell him, "You're making your mother nervous."

Amber and Wayne look surprised. They laugh. I don't get it. What's so funny about making Amber nervous?

To distract JJ from the edge of the deck, I show him how to make a rhino horn with a maple seed pod. I split it and press it onto my nose, but it won't stick. It's not green enough. I hold it on and show him my profile. "See?"

JJ is speechless.

A thought occurs to me. "You know what a rhinoceros is?" I ask.

"He knows," Amber says.

I ask JJ if he can whistle with grass. He doesn't know what I'm talking about, so I trot down the silver steps, and pick a few long blades of grass and bring them back up to the deck. Mercifully, one works on the first try. I manage a long, clear note, then a vibrato. JJ's face lights up. I feel like a magician. Even more mercifully, JJ is able, very quickly, to do it himself. He lays the green blade between his small, thick, dirty thumbs, cups his hands and blows out a triumphant shriek.

Wayne excuses himself to cut the grass. JJ runs off to show off his new trick to his more timid older brother. Amber and I stay put. Somewhere behind the house, a duet of grassy blasts and screeches rises over the drone of a lawn mower. It is a golden spring afternoon.

I'm thinking, maybe I'm the one who's paranoid, bringing my own darkness into the house with me. The dog wasn't cowering at Wayne's feet; he was leaning affectionately into his ankles. Wayne himself seems kind and willing and able, not controlling or obstructive. The kids are happy, bright-eyed, well-cared for. Clearly Amber has been a good mother to them. She glows with maternal pride.

On the way home I realize that it was the first time I'd talked to Amber without the TV. It seemed a luminous afternoon.

MAY 22, FRIDAY

A week in Florida, our turn to visit Andy's mother Agnes, who suffers from dementia. Getting on the plane, we were a pair of zombies: Andy from his surgery and me from taking care of him while performing my own surgery—cutting a hundred pages out of my new book at my agent's behest. I mailed the manuscript on the way to the airport. I could barely see straight. Andy was moving as cautiously as an old man. We got through the visit with Agnes then had three days by ourselves in Key West. The hotel was built around a large quiet garden with palms, purple-black shrubs, lizards, mossy brick paths, water splashing on stone. We slept a lot and drank the most delicious vodka tonics (maybe it was the limes?) and walked around the town.

I didn't think much about Amber. Before we left, I sent her a Mother's Day card saying that I enjoyed meeting Wayne and the boys and that she was obviously a very good mother. Claire said Amber showed it off to her.

Today, Amber calls just as I'm going out the door to visit her. She tells me that I don't need to come. She's fixed her own lunch—leftovers from Chinese takeout. (She'd been hankering for Chinese for a month or so, I think, blaming Wayne for never bringing a meal home.)

"It doesn't matter about lunch," I say. "I'd still like to visit with you. I haven't seen you in a couple weeks."

Silence at the end of the line.

"Is someone there with you? Have you already got company?"

"There's nobody here."

"Then I'd like to see you. Unless you don't feel up to it?"

"I feel okay."

Summery day, gray road dust plastering the leafy tunnel through the hollow, enormous bees drifting in through Amber's sliding doors. I shoo them out with a magazine. Amber looks different, prettier. She's wearing makeup, nicely done. The liner around her eyes emphasizes their almond-shape and gives her an exotic look. I compliment her. She tells me she's wearing her contacts—which really does make a difference. Without her goggle-like big-rims, you can see her face. She has penciled in slanting eyebrows that recall Spock of the Starship Enterprise. I notice shadows at her temples. "Is your hair growing in?" I ask.

She is reluctant to say so. The top of her head bothers her. No hair there, for sure. It's bald and shiny and white.

Her torso is bigger and rounder than ever, but her legs and arms are still stick-like. Her body suggests a child's drawing. Later in the visit, she takes out her contacts, puts her glasses back on, worries about facial hair. "Maybe it's the steroids," she speculates.

I see no facial hair from where I sit, but I offer to bring her some depilatory. She turns her head to show me a baby-fine tuft of hair growing at the nape of her neck. "Wayne doesn't like it," she says.

"Would you like me to cut it off?"

She accepts readily, gives me the scissors. I trim the tuft, put a thin curl of brown baby hair in her hand. She examines it with interest.

This time it's a real visit. She scarcely pays attention to the

TV. I tell her about the Key West scene: the six-toed cats at Hemingway's house, the crowds of tourists, the abundance of gay men. We talk about homosexuality. "It's not right," she starts out adamantly. I say I'm not sure it's a matter of right or wrong. And then she feels free to talk about a gay friend who died of AIDS.

I bring up the matter of planning for the kids' summer. Mare sent information on a Parks and Recreation day camp, but the fee schedule confused her. I go over it with her, but even when she realizes how cheap the program is, she balks because it's only half day and she needs all day. She rejects a church-run camp. "I don't know what they'll teach my boys," she objects. She tells me she once bought a book of Bible stories for them, but tossed it after JJ asked why Cain had killed Abel. He'd also asked why God had let all the people drown in the Flood. "The Bible's too violent," she declares.

Just then, Peter Jennings breaks into the commercials with an update on the latest school shooting. That morning in Oregon, a teenage boy came to school heavily armed and started shooting. Jennings reports twelve injured. Turns out the kid shot his parents to death and then went to school and shot up the gym. A couple of students brought him down while he was reloading. He asked them to shoot him.

We shake our heads and cluck and talk about families. Her father, whom she has not seen in years, is about to visit her sister. She does not want to reconcile with him, but at the same time doesn't want him to leave all his money to her sisters' children and shut her boys out. "I'll sue," she promises. The tiger in her emerging.

I ask about Wayne's family. They're local, she says. His mother died when he was an infant. He was raised by his great-grandmother, then his grandmother. He and his grandmother

lived out in a "shed at the back of the property." She makes it
sound slightly sinister, as if they were being punished.

"A shed?"

"There was no plumbing," she says. "I never figured out what
was going on there."

I think about Wayne: he lost his mother. Now family history
is repeating itself: his boys are about to lose Amber.

She talks about him playing with the kids, running around
the house with them. "He tickles them until they cry. Then the
game's over." She is disapproving. She wants Wayne to act like a
"grown-up." I wonder about the tickling: innocent play? Abusive
behavior?

She and Wayne are still at odds over chores. She's now cooking most nights. He's supposed to do the laundry, but she complains that he's behind. She opens the door to the basement to
show me a spill of dirty clothes flowing down the stairs. Not being
able to keep control of her house bothers her. When her friend
Debby doesn't clean the boys' bedroom for her, she tidies it herself. She says Wayne gets angry at her, wants her to do more. "It's
like he *blames* me for being sick."

I suppose I should have explored this with her, but I duck
instead of delving. I offer a reason for Wayne's anger. "Maybe he's
scared," I say. "He obviously likes having you take care of things
for him."

"Yes." She nods gravely. "I think that's the attraction he had
to me, as a mother." Her tone is resigned.

Is this a new thought or an old one? An end-of-life rehash-
ing or something she's lived with since the kids were born and
she put on the pounds? I remember a line from one of her
poems: "I lay beside you in the dark knowing you don't want me
anymore."

Something else she said comes back to me. It must have been

an early visit because I was asking her about the chronology of her cancer: when she was diagnosed, how long she had been fighting it. "I think it must have started when I was carrying JJ," she told me.

There's a lot of dots here between Mother and Death. Amber's mother, Wayne's mother, now Amber herself. Do I want to connect the dots and look at the picture? I don't think so.

MAY 23, SATURDAY

When "Death knocks," the skeletal fist poking out of the black sleeve doesn't belong to a woman. It's a male fist rapping on the door. The word "killer" in a headline isn't really gender-free—not yet, anyway: it evokes a "he." Maternal images of death and destruction shock us—whether it's a clip on the news of a well-groomed young mother who has killed her two-year-old or a temple carving of Kali Ma garlanded with skulls and gnawing her husband's entrails. We see mothers as life-givers, not death-dealers.

The American mom is always clean and shiny. She may not bake her own apple pie anymore, but she feeds her children cornflakes in sunny kitchens, washes dirt out of their clothes, cures their colds and coughs. Mothers of young children aren't supposed to hurt or abandon their babies. They aren't supposed to get sick and die.

This wasn't always so. A hundred years ago, mothers died regularly in childbirth. My maternal great-grandmother, Lily Lalor Crimmins, died after the youngest of her thirteen children, Clarence, was born. Granny was too young to remember. She used to speak regretfully of never having known her mother, but in the same way that people today speak of a parental divorce: her mother's death may have been key to her personal development, but it was not uncommon.

I looked up the dates. Granny was two and a half when her mother died. Lily Lalor Crimmins died in 1888. She was forty—four years older than Amber.

I'm thinking that when we actually get to death's door, numbers don't matter all that much. Dying at one hundred and two may be as hard as dying at thirty-six or thirty-nine or forty.

MRS. O'CASEY

Dies irae, dies illa
Solvet saeclum in favilla
Teste David cum Sibylla.

—from the Roman Catholic Requiem Mass

ACCORDING to the intake sheet, Mrs. O'Casey was one hundred and two years old. I blinked in surprise. But no, there was no mistake. Nikki Hill confirmed it with some delight. I thought, *Well, this should be easy enough. A hundred and two. She must be ready to go.*

According to Nikki, Mrs. O'Casey was blind and extremely deaf ("You have to really *scream* at her," Nikki warned). She was also difficult to understand (her cancer had eaten away part of her jaw). She was in her own home, bedridden and incontinent. She had outlived her only son, but had enough money left to pay for a caregiver. "She's an educated woman," Nikki said. "She's neat."

I imagined a fragile, wizened old woman waiting for release.

Her house was a large Victorian in severe disrepair. It had been at least twenty years (Mrs. O'Casey would have been eighty-something) since the house had been painted. The gutters sagged, the front steps were collapsing, unpruned shrubs hid the porch. The caregiver ushered me into a front parlor where Mrs. O'Casey was installed in her bed. The floor was linoleum, a '30s rose pattern, and on the wall, framed sepia photos, the faces bleached to cream. I approached the bed feeling reverential.

"Mrs. O'Casey?" I called loudly.

She was a heavyset woman with half her face in bandages. What was left of her jaw was square. Her wrists were as thick as ax handles. I took her hand. "MRS. O'CASEY," I yelled.

Suddenly I was falling on top of her. She had latched onto my wrist and jerked me into bed with her. The impact of my fall released a stink of urine from her mattress. I gagged, found my footing and tried to pull back off the bed, but she would not let me go. The woman was as strong as an ox.

We screamed at each other, nose to nose, for maybe fifteen minutes. During this exchange, I learned that she was a graduate of Smith College, that she had weathered two husbands, a career as a teacher, and seven wars.

"SEVEN?" I bellowed.

She named them, beginning with the Spanish American War. *The Spanish American War?* When I got home, I looked it up. 1898. The United States had gone to war to liberate Cuba from Spain. (My grandmother's older brother Martin had dropped out of the University of Virginia to join the fight. He had signed on with Teddy Roosevelt's "Rough Riders," but never made it to Cuba: when his regiment shipped out from Tampa, Florida, he was left behind to tend the horses—much to his disappointment.)

Subsequent visits to Mrs. O'Casey made me proud to live in a small town. Her dinners were provided by Wynn's Restaurant on Main Street and delivered, every day at noon, by a pair of deputies from the sheriff's department. Their round of duties included checks on elderly shut-ins and Mrs. O'Casey was a favorite. The deputies arranged a birthday cake for her one hundred third birthday. They presented her with a new sweater to wear in bed. But most of all, every day, they arrived, girded in their gun belts, bearing white Styrofoam containers from Wynn's.

These dinners were the high point of Mrs. O'Casey's day. She devoured Wynn's fried chicken and pork chops, his apple sauce, mashed potatoes, sweet potatoes, corn, cole slaw, beans, biscuits, and lemon pies. When I visited, she would take me through each meal. It finally occurred to me: *this one-hundred-and-three-year-old woman, this blind, deaf, barely comprehensible, incontinent, immobile, clear-minded, muscular, ancient woman WANTS TO LIVE.* She had no intention of surrendering. She was desperately holding onto her life. If age had anything to do with the will to live, she might have been twenty-three, not a hundred and three.

As it turned out, Mrs. O'Casey's age was a lie. When our nurse gave her the choice of being moved into a nursing home or into a hospital bed in her own house, she choose the latter. She was moved into the clean bed and the reeking mattress was carted away. Underneath it, there was stash of money and two birth certificates—one real and one fake. Via a screaming match, I learned (if I understood correctly) that at age sixteen, she had applied for a job that required her to be seventeen—hence the fake certificate. She actually was not a hundred and three. She was "only" a hundred and two.

I was not present at her death. When she finally sank into her coma, a middle-aged nephew was notified. He arrived from a distant state in a rusting, finned Oldsmobile, made a beeline for his aunt's desk, and spent the deathwatch poring through her check-book—"putting her affairs in order," he explained to the faithful deputies. They were, of course, suspicious, but there was nothing to be done. She had named him as next of kin. I don't remember whether or not he went to the expense of a funeral.

I walk in and find Amber asleep on top of the bed (neatly made-up). I'm reminded of a hopeful, exhausted child who's fallen asleep waiting for a party. She's wearing makeup, a turquoise blue striped top I haven't seen before, and blue socks to match.

She tells me Wayne took her to Kmart to buy a birthday present for her friend Debby—a portable CD player. "She's wanted one for the longest time." But she worries that she's picked the wrong model.

I try to visualize her in Kmart. Was she wearing her wig? Using her walker? "You're feeling stronger," I marvel. "That's great!"

"I'm doing everything except the laundry." She is both pleased by the improvement and angered by Wayne's insistence that she take back charge of the household. "He expects me to do everything. He won't do anything about the kids' summer." She's been in touch with "a woman here on the mountain" who will sit for the boys in her home, but Wayne objects to the expense. "He's the one who's run us into debt. He didn't have to put in this toilet. He didn't have to go build a new deck."

She says he's not happy with his job but if he quits, he'll lose the insurance that covers her care. "He blames me for trapping him in a job he doesn't like."

Yesterday he called her from work and said she had to get someone to pick up the kids from school. She told him Debby couldn't do it and he swore at her over the phone. She found another friend to pick up the kids and keep them till he got there, but he showed up an hour late at the friend's house. "He didn't get them home till seven. I had dinner on the table at six."

She went ahead and ate alone and put the rest of the meal in the oven for them. "I was feeling pretty snippy," she admitted. When they finally came home, she stayed in her bedroom. After they'd finished eating and the kids were doing homework, she came out and confronted Wayne: "Where were you?"

"He blew up at me. 'I'm tired of all your shit.' Like that. In front of the kids. I told him, 'Well, you won't have to put up with me that much longer, I'll be dead soon enough.' Then I saw the kids' faces. That bothers me. I wish I hadn't said it."

The boys keep a careful distance from her. "They're worried about getting the cancer bug from me. They won't drink from my glass. They don't want me to hug them."

She thinks perhaps the reason she's feeling better is that she needs to be around to look after the boys. She toys with the idea of trying a new experimental treatment.

At the same time, she does not want to lose her hospice benefit. She feels she won't live long. She says her ribs and her back hurt.

I tell her she needs to stay on top of her pain, to discuss it with Claire.

She worries about becoming addicted to painkillers.

I tell her that narcotics taken for physical pain are not addictive.

She had a "drug phase" after high school. "I got in with a bad crowd," she confesses. This was in Arlington, where she lived with her mother and her stepfather. After the death of her stepfather, her mother moved out to her cabin on the mountain. A year later, Amber joined her and "got herself straightened out."

She asks me to go into her closet to find a maroon gym bag for her. It is full of old photos. She spreads them out on the bed and shows me her baby pictures (gawky and bald, with only a bit more fuzz than now), her grade-school pictures. She is prim and pretty—not cute (her nose is too long for cute). In one picture, her eyes are puffy. ("I spent the night before crying my eyes out over someone. Or maybe it was allergies.")

I pick up a color eight-by-ten of a young woman in a show-girl's costume: net stockings, gold sequins, a plumed headdress. "Is this you?" I ask, trying not to sound incredulous. She is stunning. I recognize her long legs, but not the supple line of her slim back, the proud, confident tilt of her chin. Her arm is raised in a triumphant ta-daa.

She tells me that when she was fifteen and sixteen, she belonged to a high school troupe of jazz dancers. The portrait was taken at the high point of her career: a competition in Atlantic City.

"You were gorgeous!" I feel as if I've discovered gold.

"If I'd kept it up, maybe I wouldn't have gotten into a bad crowd," she says flatly.

I can't take my eyes off the picture. "You should leave this one out," I tell her. "Show it to your boys. Have they ever seen it?"

She shrugs. "I never liked the way I looked. I was never satisfied with my figure."

Well, we all know about that.

She fishes through the photos and finds a folded sheet of typing paper. She hands it to me. I open it up. It's a poem. The title is "Last Instructions." It's been typed on an old manual machine with a weak ribbon.

The gist of it is: When I'm dead and cold, laid out on a sheet (the first part is pretty clinical), give my heart to someone who's had pain in their heart, give my eyes to someone who's had trouble seeing beauty, and so on, going through all the organs. The final lines are something like: Give all my faults to the Devil and all my goodness to God.

I look up from it, a little shocked.

"I don't know where it came from," she says. "Maybe it was my mother's." She pushes the photos away. "They're making me dizzy."

I put them back in the closet for her.

On the drive home, I decide to buy her an album. If she doesn't want to make a tape for the boys, perhaps she can put together a visual history for them. Perhaps I can get her to pick out the photos, dictate labels to me.

NELL

By means of an image we are often able to hold onto our lost belongings. But it is the desperateness of losing which picks the flowers of memory, binds the bouquet.

—Colette, *Mes Apprentissages*

NELL and her husband Carl were in their mid-eighties. They both came from farming families, but he had spent his working life in Front Royal's rayon factory whose brick smokestacks punctuated the view through their picture window. In their backyard, they had once tended a farm-size garden. They had also planted fruit trees. She talked about the jams and jellies and pies she had made with their own plums and apples and cherries. He talked about how hard it was to nurse the trees along all those years, then see them grow old and diseased. He had cut them all down, all but a last plum tree. "It don't even give enough for a pie," he said sadly. He shook his head and his sorrow seemed to fill the room.

Nell, however, was impatient with his grief. "It sure is pretty in the spring," she reminded him sharply.

———

They were frail, white, and thin-lipped, but he was handsome with longish steel-gray hair (slickly combed back), and she, though she had only wisps of hair left, was beautiful. Her features had a chiseled delicacy that gave her an air of refinement: when she spoke, her country twang came as a surprise.

I used to look at her and wonder if, in the springtime of her own life, she had been as beautiful as she was now. I thought perhaps not. I imagined her as plump and pretty in the fashion of the '40s, with red lipstick and permed dark hair. Now age had dried her up, bleached away all color; her skin looked like tissue paper that has been crumpled up and smoothed out. Old age, however, also revealed the aristocracy of her bones. In the afternoon sunlight, her soft wisps of hair backlit silver, her skin almost translucent, she could have passed for an ancient queen.

One afternoon I asked if I could take her picture. I was thinking black and white, the kind of photo that might hang in a gallery. I hadn't taken anything but Instamatic snapshots for the past twenty years, but with a face like Nell's, I felt I could launch, if not a thousand ships, then a new career for myself. To my surprise, she refused.

"Why not?"

"I don't like the way I look."

"But I think you look beautiful!" I protested.

She snorted. "I look like a corpse." From a stack of romance novels (the steamy variety) on her bedside table, she pulled out a colored snapshot and handed it to me. It had been taken at Christmastime, just after she had been admitted to hospice. It showed her lying back in bed amid a litter of bright wrappings and ribbons. She was wearing a plump gray wig. Her eyes were half-mast, her skin yellow. In fact, she looked dead.

"That's not a good picture," I agreed. "I think I could do a whole lot better than that."

"No," she said.

I didn't want to let it go. "How would you *like* to look?" I persisted.

She thought about it a minute. "Like I'm seventy," she decided.

Nell died attended by her husband Carl, their daughter, and their grandson. I went to the visitation at the funeral home. I was glad to see that the long, carpeted room was crowded with friends. At one end Nell was laid out in her coffin. I went up to the coffin. People gave me space.

She was wearing the shiny gray wig I'd seen in the Christmas snapshot (to my eye, it looked like a prop for *Saturday Night Live*) and her face had the bloom of a serious makeup job. I searched for the fragile, ancient queen I had seen in the afternoon sunlight and couldn't find her.

At the other end of the room, Carl sat on a small settee receiving friends. Again, people made room for me. I offered condolences. He nodded. "They cleaned her up right good," he said proudly.

"Yes," I agreed.

MAY 29, FRIDAY

I get through to Mare on the phone and report on the boys' fear of "catching" cancer. She says Amber came up for reevaluation yesterday at the team meeting. Claire discussed Amber's improved condition and Dr. Houck suggested that she come to his office for a visit. "We need a better idea of what's going on physically with her," Mare says. "After she sees Houck, if she's still in the program, I'll address the matter of talking to the kids."

JUNE 1, MONDAY

I call Amber to offer to drive her over to Winchester for her doctor's appointment but she knows nothing about it, Mare hadn't gotten to her, so I end up telling her about the team's recommendation. She's suspicious. "Are you trying to get rid of me?"

I remind her that she's been in the program for two months. "It's just a routine review of your case," I say, passing on what I'd gotten from Mare. "We're concerned with where you are." I pause and add a thought of my own. "I would think you'd want to know. It might help you plan too."

Silence.

"We're not going to abandon you," I promise. "Even if you don't need the aides anymore, the nurses will keep coming. Maybe just not so often. And I'll keep coming to see you."

"What's the doctor going to do? He's not going to know anything just from looking at me. Is he going to do more tests?"

"Amber, all I know is that Dr. Houck suggested you make an appointment with him."

"If I go, Wayne should go with me. To hear what he says."

"You'll make the appointment?"

"I might wait till school's out."

Then Mare calls me. She's talked to Amber and worries whether Amber's insurance will cover another visit to the doctor.

"She really opened up to me," Mare says. Amber told her how she had cooked pancakes for the boys' breakfast and they told her that Wayne's pancakes were better than hers—which hurt her feelings. Mare feels there's a lot of issues that need to be talked about with Brett and JJ. "They need straight knowledge about what's happening and what might happen, to both them and their mother." She says she'll try to set up a visit with them after school lets out.

She didn't come out and say so, but I have the feeling that while she's willing to work with the boys, she's written Amber off in a kind of social worker's triage. "She's very complex," Mare says, choosing her words carefully. "She seems to be distorting somewhat."

"You think she's paranoid?"

She balks at the word.

We agree that Amber is super-sensitive—and afraid.

After we hang up, I look up *paranoia* in the dictionary on my desk. "Usually chronic psychosis characterized by delusions of persecution or of grandeur . . ."

Amber doesn't fit this. She doesn't think we are out to get her. She's worried about being shut out—by hospice, by her husband, and by her sons.

JUNE 2, TUESDAY

Long phone call with Claire. Amber's hedging, her whiny indeci-
sion annoys and frustrates Claire. She sees Amber as "extremely
manipulative." Yesterday she confronted Amber and insisted that
she go to see Dr. Houck. "I told her that I can't document her
need for hospice. She's improving physically, she says she's in no
pain, then she reverses and says she feels changes!" Claire was
indignant. "She's not popping all those pills for pain, Christine.
She's using them to feel good."

Surprise, surprise. But what a mess—and after I had told
Amber that we wouldn't cut her loose. You'd think the prospect
of being discharged from hospice would be cause for hope, if not
celebration, but in Amber's case, I can see only disaster: escalat-
ing fights with Wayne, the kids lost and in pain.

Just thinking about her life makes her dying seem luxurious:
friends to clean your house and watch your children; strangers
bearing home-cooked meals and expensive chocolates; hospice
workers to change your sheets and massage your feet, to listen to
your life and dope your pain. All this love and attention and sorrow instead of, what? Washing up and picking up and shopping
and cooking—all on a tight budget, so there's the constant picking and choosing and scrimping. Add in a disease-distorted body,
the probability of permanent brain damage, a fed-up husband,
and rejecting sons.

The configuration of her household is the same as mine: one
man, two boys. I know what it feels like to be excluded by the
ordinary bonds of maleness. It's supposed to be psychologically
healthy for sons to align themselves with their father, but I
remember bleak, gray patches of loneliness and the sense of being
utterly replaceable. Amber's excluded not only by the accident of
her gender, but by the accident of her disease. Twice over, she is
existentially Other. How do you cope with *that?*

Really, her death seems the easiest solution—for me, anyway. I make her a nice album to leave for her boys, she dies, all parties are sad and relieved. Hospice has done its thing and we all congratulate ourselves on having muddled through such a "difficult case."

JUNE 4, THURSDAY

Amber spiffed up, contacts in, makeup on, upbeat mood. She thinks her hair is growing in and in fact, there's a five-o'clock shadow on her head—except for a shiny white stripe, three inches wide that bisects her skull and ends in that odd little tuft of hair above her nape. I urge her to see Houck. "Given your improvement, maybe you'll be a candidate for more treatment."

Well, she's not improving, her ribs hurt, she's dizzy all the time.

"What would it be like for you if you did go into remission?" I ask.

"You mean, all my hair in, my figure back?"

It's not what I mean, but I'm curious. "Yes," I say.

She looks at me as if I'm crazy. "Why—" she flounders, as if the mere thought is too good to even consider. "Why, it would be wonderful!" There is a note of sheer joy in her voice.

Exactly who is the one here half in love with easeful death?!

JUNE 11, THURSDAY

Amber brighter than ever, the shadow on her scalp a bit darker. I find her lounging on the bed, soaps on, big orange cat beside her. Her languid posture and the pile of blue-and-green paisley pillows behind suggest an odalisque. The sliding door is open and black flies bump off the ceiling. We swing blue plastic swatters at them while we talk. An especially annoying one irritates me out of my chair. I stalk it, swatter poised. I land a satisfying slap on the TV, but miss. Finally I nail it on the bedspread and go, "*Yesss!*"

Amber observes me with interest.

I wonder how killing flies fits into the hospice ethic.

Saturday, Wayne took off to the NASCAR races with his chums. ("I guess it did him some good," Amber reflects benignly.) While he was gone, and the boys were over at a friend's house, she was napping on the bed and her orange cat brought in a baby rabbit. The rabbit's shrieking woke her up. She rescued it from the cat's jaws and made a nest for it with a towel in the portable potty in her room. The cat, however, went bananas hearing the thing scratching against the plastic sides of the potty, so she transferred it to a large kitchen pot and put it in the bathroom with the door shut to keep out the cat. She mixed up a formula of milk and honey but couldn't manage to get it to swallow any. When Wayne came home late that night, he was able to feed it, and in the morning it was still alive.

Amber's tone is flat as usual, but I sit up. Suddenly, the lines of the room seem sharper. The story is no longer a slightly tedious account of her afternoon. It's shifted into the magical dimensions of myth and metaphor. The baby rabbit strikes me emblematic. I ask her about it. She tells me it was only an inch or two long, but its eyes were open, its ears perfectly formed, and it was covered with soft brown fur. "It had a small white patch on its head," she adds.

The next day she called the vet who gave her numbers of various wildlife groups. One authority said rabbits were lactose intolerant and suggested trying soy milk. Someone else warned against handling it too much. Another told her that if she could keep it alive for a week, it would survive on its own in the wild. She felt overwhelmed by the task and gave the rabbit to a neighbor. "She cradled it, held it, took it home with her. She was very tender with it." She shows me, gently rocking cupped hands against her breast. Despite the neighbor's efforts, the rabbit died that night.

The end of the story shocks me. Is the baby rabbit a portend? If so, what does it mean?

Amber's own questions are more matter-of-fact. She wonders why it died. Was it her milk-and-honey formula? Had the neighbor woman handled it too much? Amber doesn't blame the woman. But clearly, she had tender feelings of her own for the infant rabbit. She had wanted it to live.

She seems to have things together. She made an appointment with Houck. She's also lined up a sitter for the boys for the summer. She's concerned about hiring a stranger over the phone and plans to visit the sitter with Wayne and check her out in person, but the specter of child abuse nags at her. She tells me that in Arlington, she knew several girls who had been sexually abused. She tells me how the father of one of her friends had come into her room at night and tried to "get his hands between my legs." Her friend had slept through it—or pretended to—and Amber had threatened the man with waking up his wife.

She also talks about doing drugs when she was a teenager. "Perhaps if my stepfather hadn't died, I'd have been okay. But after his death, my mother kind of withdrew. She used to come out here to the cabin by herself, leaving me alone with my friends."

"What kind of drugs?" I ask.

"Grass and acid." She had no problems with acid, she said, but grass used to make her "kind of paranoid."

One of her sisters has been in touch with their father. During their visit, he kept making cracks about how fat the sister was. So now the sister wants nothing to do with him. Amber says he used to do the same thing to her. She doesn't want to see him but she toys with the idea of reconciliation. She says she tried writing him a letter, then crumpled it up because it had gotten "nasty." (From things she's said about her father during other visits, I have the feeling that even though she talks as if she had tried to write the letter this past week, it actually happened years ago—an example of what Mare calls "distorting"?)

Unlike her own father, she trusts Wayne as a good parent to the boys. "The only thing he couldn't stand was if one of them would turn out to be homosexual." Again, she mentions her gay friend who had died of AIDS. His partner of fifteen years had "given up" after his death and died shortly thereafter. "I always thought it was kind of romantic," she says. But in the next breath she is judgmental: "I don't think it's right."

She seems to be reviewing, in a half-conscious way, all the possible dangers for Brett and JJ: child abuse, drugs, homosexuality.

Meanwhile, the TV makes its rainbow noise. A young man with doe-like eyes stares blankly at us then faints on a ruby red and sapphire blue Persian carpet. Some episodes ago, he emerged from a coma with disturbing psychic visions of the future; since then he has been literally assaulted by his newfound gift. It knocks him out at odd moments. "I don't think I'd like that to happen to me," Amber remarks.

I remember her seizures.

"Do you believe that can really happen?" she presses.

"You mean suddenly being able to see the future?"

"Yes."

"Well," I say cautiously, "some people report having a prophetic dream or vision when someone they are close to is in danger or has died. But it seems to be a one-shot deal. They aren't plagued with it like our handsome hero."

She sits up, suddenly alert. "Yes. Something weird happened the morning my mother died. I woke up hearing her voice. She said, 'I haven't made the house over to you.' It was like she was right there. I wondered, 'What's that about?' and went back to sleep."

Hours later she found her mother dead.

"She told me she was going to give me the house. But she never got around to putting it in her will so it went to the three of us, me and my sisters. Wayne and I had to buy out their shares."

Amber's story makes me think of my patient Lucy whose voice I heard about half an hour after she died. Being with Lucy during her death was an amazing experience—one of the most profound of my life—but I am not sure exactly how to tell Amber about it. Even if I can find the right words, is it appropriate to talk to her about a former patient's death? I hesitate and the opening closes. Amber is back into her soap.

LUCY

The meeting of two personalities is like the contact of two chemical substances: if there is any
reaction, both are transformed.

—Carl Jung, *Modern Man in Search of a Soul*

LUCY Wood reminded me of my grandmother. Neither their
looks nor their lives had any similarity, but both Lucy and my
grandmother would light up at the sight of me and shower me
with happy compliments. If I felt a little fraudulent, it did not
diminish the pleasure of their praise.

Lucy was a native of Front Royal, a widow who had enjoyed a
long marriage to an orchardist in the next county. A few years
before his death, they had moved back into town, into the house
in which she had grown up. As a widow she had taken hospice
training with the idea of working as a patient-care volunteer, but
she never did get to have a patient. She was diagnosed with colon
cancer not long after she completed her training. She fought her
disease for three years, then became a hospice patient herself in
August, 1995. Everyone, including Lucy herself, believed she was
at death's door.

Her daughter Frances Charles, who lived in Alabama, took a
leave of absence from her job to care for her mother. However, as

so often happens when a patient comes home to die, Lucy improved dramatically under Frances's meticulous and loving care. From being completely helpless and bedridden, Lucy could now sit up in a chair and even walk to the bathroom.

She lived on Blue Ridge Avenue, a street lined with tall maples and houses built in the last century. Lucy's house had never been grand (after her mother's divorce, the family lived in "reduced circumstances") but it had high ceilings, a formal front parlor, and small fireplaces for burning coal. Frances had installed a hospital bed for her in the sunlit dining room. At the side of the backyard, close to the house, there was an old pear tree. Lucy remembered picking its fruit as a child.

I wish she had let me tape her. I loved the way she talked. Her voice was soft and quick and Southern; she was given to genteel, old-fashioned usages but delivered them perkily, with an almost flirtatious irony. She had an endless stock of stories (I don't think I ever heard the same one twice) and she would chatter on and on about her family and friends. If at times my attention wandered, her punch lines always made me sit up. At times I felt I had landed inside *Fried Green Tomatoes*. Lucy's stories dealt with the sadness and pain of ordinary life, but there was a kind of humorous amusement in her voice, so that I thought the end (if she would ever get to it) was going to be funny. Usually it wasn't. A neighbor ended up dead under the wheels of his tractor; a betrayed wife ended up penniless. "But that's terrible!" I would protest, and she would give me a little nod of satisfaction.

The story I remember best was about her grandfather, a captain in the Confederate army, who upon coming home from the war, threw his saber away into a cornfield and vowed that he would never fight again. He went on to become a preacher and was considered something of a misfit by his family. Lucy remembered his cavalry officer's sash, a long length of red silk, fringed at the ends. As a child, she used to wear it in Memorial Day parades.

Someone would wrap it round and round the waist of her white dress and she would proudly march down Main Street.

Another story from her childhood featured a box of chocolates. On one of Lucy's birthdays, a wealthy cousin came to visit and brought her a box of chocolates as a present. It was an unimaginable luxury. An entire *box* of chocolates! But, Lucy remembered guiltily, "I never offered one to anybody." Instead, she took them up to bed with her that night and ate them all before morning. "I was so ashamed!" she declared. Her childish greed bothered her still. At the same time, the thought of those long-ago birthday chocolates made her mouth water.

She enjoyed talking about food, even though she suffered from almost constant nausea and frequent bouts of vomiting. She blamed this condition not on her cancer, but on her doctors. After surgery to remove the cancer from her bowel, she had undergone radiation treatments which, she said, had given her abdomen second-degree burns and had "microwaved" her insides. Her skin had "turned the color of charcoal" and her intestines had "twisted all up" so that she had to undergo three more operations to remove the blockages. I have no idea how accurate Lucy was in her account of her medical trials. Finding out the literal truth was not my job; acknowledging her anger and loss was.

Whatever the cause, when I met her she was able to swallow only clear liquids. She was slowly starving to death, and in her starving, to my surprise, she feasted on memories of meals past. She would look at the little cups of broth and tea and Jell-O on her tray and recall, vividly and fondly, the food she had enjoyed as a farm wife: hush puppies "all crispy on the outside and soft and warm on the inside"; "rabbit in gravy" and home-cured hams; a meal of shrimp at a roadhouse that "looked like an old barn and had a sign that said EATS." She talked about baking six different kinds of cakes at Christmastime to have on hand for visitors: chocolate layer, spice, coconut—I don't remember them all, but fruit cake wasn't among them. Sometimes I'd ask her how she had cooked one thing or other, but she had no interest in cooking, only the end result.

After a month under Frances's care, Lucy still had not died. Frances had to return to her job in Alabama. She hired a live-in caregiver whom I will called Jacqueline. Jacqueline was able and experienced and known to the family; she had taken care of a relative during his last days. However, as Frances delicately put it, she "tended to inflict her religion on people." Lucy was more blunt: "She's a Jesus freak."

Jacqueline was not deterred by the fact that her patient already believed in Jesus. Lucy was a contented member of the Presbyterian church and enjoyed her minister's frequent visits. Jacqueline, however, was determined to convert Lucy to *her* Jesus. She never missed an opportunity to preach.

Although dependent on Jacqueline for every physical need, Lucy fought back. She made irreverent comments, took a comically irreligious stance. Her resistance only fueled Jacqueline's sense of mission. So Lucy switched tactics: whenever Jacqueline started into her spiel, Lucy would pull the sheet up over her head and literally play dead. "I'm determined not to get into it with her," she told me.

Even now, I wonder at the scene. What did Lucy think about under her sheet? Was she steaming? Did she pray for deliverance?

By September, the situation had become untenable. Frances, who had been driving back and forth between Alabama and Virginia, tried to find another caregiver, but the search was fruitless and Lucy elected to move into a nursing home. "Frances needs to get on with her life," she told me. Her unspoken and unflinching corollary was, "It's time for me to die." She did not want to take anything with her, but Frances and I insisted. The thought of her dying in an empty room was simply too bleak for us. Frances placed a collection of family photographs on her dresser and hung a favorite print on the wall, a reproduction of Renoir's *The Luncheon of the Boating Party*. (Bivie Peterson and I had connected through the same painting and when I first visited Lucy, I was surprised to find it on the wall opposite her bed. Lucy didn't think it was much of coincidence. "Isn't it everybody's favorite?" she asked.)

On an expanse of dry brown lawn outside the nursing home, Frances and I chipped out five holes in the cementlike soil and planted a cluster of bright yellow chrysanthemums where Lucy could see them from her bed. Then Frances said good-bye and drove back to Alabama. Lucy died before the flowers finished blooming.

By the time she moved into the nursing home, Lucy was so emaciated that her head looked too heavy for her neck, like an overlarge fruit on a twig. It amazed me that she had the strength to hold it up at all and when she was racked by the dry heaves, I had the queasy feeling that her neck might snap.

The failure to control Lucy's nausea, I learned later, was due to lack of interface between hospice, the facility's nurses, and Lucy's doctor. Although both Lucy's nurses at the facility and the doctor believed themselves supportive of hospice, neither seemed to have a practical grasp of what end-of-life pain control and comfort measures entailed. This lack of understanding also resulted in Lucy being catheterized as her kidneys began to shut down two days before her death. Since all Lucy's tissues had shrunken, it took numerous painful tries over a twenty-four-hour period to insert a catheter into her. Lucy called hospice, but the nursing home declined our nurse's offer of help and our nurse did not feel she could insist on calling the shots. Lucy also called Frances in Alabama. (Since Lucy's goal was not to "be a nuisance" to Frances, her call for help was a true measure of her desperation.) Frances tried in vain to contact Lucy's doctor by phone. Eventually she reached one of his colleagues, but he only reinforced the order for the catheter.

I knew nothing of this as it happened, but chanced to visit shortly after the facility's nurses had obtained a child-size catheter and finally managed to insert it. Lucy was extremely agitated. A kind-faced nurse wearing a pretty cerise sweater over her whites was trying to soothe her. Both Lucy and the nurse looked relieved to see me, as if I, by virtue of my hospice badge, could rescue them. Although I did not sort out what had happened until later, it was clear that Lucy felt betrayed and violated. "I don't want any tubes prolonging my life," she kept repeating.

"But it's just a drainage tube," I tried to reassure her.

"When will they unplug me from it?" she challenged.

"They won't," I said flatly. I told her that it was like her colostomy bag; she would die with it in her. "It won't prolong anything," I promised. The staff nurse backed me up. Still, Lucy refused to buy the catheter as a "comfort measure."

No small wonder. Nonetheless, as I listened, she gradually calmed down. She said that she felt like a "dried-up old leaf, high up on a tree, waiting to be blown off." She had used this metaphor before. It seemed a wonderfully poetic evocation of the difficulty of waiting for an unknown moment—a moment that would pitch her into the Unknowable. I had imagined a sole leaf, its edges curling, soundlessly breaking loose and floating down through still autumn air. Now, however, as Lucy lay frustrated and angry in her nursing home bed, I saw the leaf clinging tenaciously to a bare branch as it bobbed and spun and quivered in a relentless wind.

Certainly Lucy had not anticipated such a struggle. "My doctor promised I wouldn't suffer at the end," she told me. "He said I could just drift off to sleep." She raised an ironic eyebrow. "That's what he said."

———

That evening, Andy and I went to a friend's house for dinner and on the way, Andy obligingly detoured to the nursing home and waited in the car while I dashed in to check on Lucy. She was resting peacefully. Thanks to the room's coral-colored walls and a shaded lamp on the dresser, the light was soft and rosy. I put new batteries in the tape recorder I'd lent her, put in a tape of Beethoven sonatas for her, and said I had to run. She thanked me for all I'd done. For a moment, I thought this was our usual mutual admiration dance, a ritual that ended every visit. Lucy would thank me and tell me how wonderful I was, and I would ignore her praise and tell her how I enjoyed being with her. But this time it was different. Perhaps my ear caught a note of finality in her voice. Instead of going into my dance, I simply accepted her thanks and I told her that I would always remember her. I asked if I could give her a kiss, and she said yes, so I leaned over and kissed her forehead. I told her that I had houseguests arriving Saturday, the next day, but that I'd come back to visit on Sunday after they left.

"I'll bring my sewing and some tapes. You won't have to talk to me. I'll just sit and listen to music with you."

"That would be nice." Her voice was contented.

"I've also left my name and phone number with the nurses. I asked them to call me if, uh, anything happens."

She protested, "You've already done so much for me. I'm just fine. I don't want to bother you anymore than I already have."

I took a breath and blurted out, "I don't want you to die alone. I don't want you to be afraid."

My words hung between us in the lamplight.

"I don't think I'll be afraid," she said simply. She thought about it for a moment, then added, "I think it will just be like—a shock."

She met my eyes. I nodded.

She'd had some morphine, I think. She closed her eyes before I was out the door.

Saturday night, we drove over the mountain with our house-guests for dinner at a country inn. Lovely food, abundant wine, the company of much-loved friends nudged Lucy from the front of my mind. By the time we got home it was eleven and I was sleepy and pleasantly fuzzy with wine. As I got out of the car, I said sincerely to Andy, "It *really* would be nice if there was no message for me on the machine."

But of course there was. The nursing home had called to say that it looked as if Lucy would not last much longer. I made a thermos of extra strong tea, grabbed some tapes and my sewing, and drove off. On the way down our hill, I was startled out of my skin by a large animal running across the road in front of my headlights. I jammed on the brakes and narrowly missed hitting it. For a second I thought it was a huge dog. Then I realized it was a bear, black as the night itself. Its blackness made it hard to see, but my headlights caught its brown footpads—uncannily human-looking—as it ran off into the woods. Definitely no dog! Suddenly I was wide-awake, tingling with adrenalin. I had not seen a bear around our house for several years. They were rare enough that the sight of one always seemed magical—and this bear even more so. Driving off in the night to attend Lucy's death had its own drama: I felt as if a veil were about to be lifted. Seeing a bear cross my path was like a trumpet blast.

Since the dawn of human consciousness, bears have been associated with sacred power; they have the mysterious ability to "die" during winter hibernation and resurrect from the ground in the spring. Shamans of many cultures derived supernatural power through a connection with the spirit of the bear and in early Christian iconography, the bear appears as a stand-in for Christ. The black bear that appeared to me, however, was so much its individual animal self that, at the time, I didn't think of it as a sign of renewal and rebirth. I simply connected to its power. I felt that whatever happened that night, the basic, grounding energy of *bear-ness* was there for me. I could summon it up, hold in my belly, and Lucy and I would be protected in its shadow.

At the nursing home, everyone was helpful and kind. Lucy's neighbor Libby had been sitting with her since five in the afternoon and the nurses had brought her a foot-high stack of magazines. It was now 1:30 A.M. Libby offered to stay; she didn't want Lucy to be alone. I told her that I was planning to stay the night, and after we'd talked a while, she left.

I settled in with my needlepoint. I inserted a tape of Mozart's clarinet concerto into the little recorder on Lucy's bedside table and turned the volume very low. I let it play through several times, but the tape had been home-dubbed by a friend and had Wagner's "Ride of the Valkeries" at the end, which sounded too screechy (not to say overblown) for the occasion, so I switched to other tapes I'd brought along. Although I knew which composers she liked, I have to say the idea of playing deejay to her death gave me pause.

Her hearing remained sharp until the end. At once point she heard me talking to one of the nurses and opened her eyes. "Oh," she said, "I didn't know you were here." Her eyes weren't really focusing and I felt that she couldn't see me very well, if at all, but had recognized me by my voice. I told her I that I was going to sit with her and play a few tapes and she made a sweet, tiny little smile.

Early on she asked about Frances.

"I talked to her before I drove out here," I said. "She's planning to arrive on Monday."

No response.

"Do you want Frances here now?" I asked. "Do you want me to call her back?"

"No," she said, very firmly.

Later, when the nurse asked about her children, I mentioned that her son was in London. Lucy said, "Arabia." She said it twice.

I said to the nurse, "I know he goes to the Middle East on business a lot." Later, I learned that her son was, in fact, about to leave London for Saudi Arabia.

I didn't talk much to her. When she was restless, I told her not to worry, that everything was taken care of. Several times I told her that her children loved her and that they knew how much she loved them. But mainly I felt that I should be quiet. She seemed very concentrated, as if focusing on an internal labor. I didn't want to interrupt. I had the persistent fantasy that if I talked to her, she might break out of her process and sit up and start chatting away in her gentle little sing-song. I never had the sense that she was "out of it"—rather than she was consciously "in it."

Her bouts of retching bothered me. The nurse said her anti-nausea medication wasn't due. By doctor's orders, she could have it only every six hours, but it was clear she would be dead before the next allowable dose. I thought about making a fuss, about calling Frances, calling hospice, rising the doctor to get the order changed. But then it wouldn't be peaceful in the room anymore. Lucy's discomfort seemed to come and go in waves. Was quelling her nausea higher on the comfort list than peace and quiet? I don't know. I chose peace and quiet.

The last half hour or so I was with Lucy, I turned off the

music. Somehow we were beyond Mozart. Her breathing was very faint and I wanted to hear it. Now and then she'd show a small restlessness, a frown, a slight shift of shoulder. Once she threw out her arm, a skeletal flail. She was so thin. If the slight hoop of her wedding ring hadn't been taped on, it would have flown off.

Very lightly, with the tips of my fingers, I soothed her forehead. I told her that she would soon be free. Experimentally, I tried matching my breath to hers, then decided nope, I'm not going there.

It was painful to see her. Her lips were white, her tongue was beige, her gasps tiny. I shut my eyes and said silent Hail Marys over and over. This wasn't so much a *Help me* as an attempt to establish a connection to the sacred.

"Hail Mary, full of grace, the Lord is with thee." It was comforting, this mantra from my past. And intellectually satisfying: a feminine evocation, recited in the circles of the rosary. But the last line transcended both religious nostalgia and feminist convictions. *"Pray for us now and at the hour of our death."* Saying that beside Lucy, perching on the edge of my chair, feeling the rail of her bed hard under my armpit as I held her hand, the words zinged in my head. *"Now and at the hour of our death."*

At my convent boarding school on the Connecticut shore, the "Now" had included nuns in black veils, Latin declensions and sunlight on Long Island Sound. The "hour of our (i.e., *my*) death" had lain some time in the far mysteries of the future. But at Lucy's bedside, Present and Future (along with the Past when I used to say the words) had all conjoined. The *now* and the *then* and the *future* "hour of our death" had all converged into the same moment. I was at a still point, at the center of time.

I stopped holding her hand. Maybe it was too bony and frail for my comfort. We'd never held hands before, just a light touch at hello and good-bye. I don't remember that she ever really grasped my hand, not until that catheter business when she was so anxious. Maybe hand-holding is something for the living, a contact. Maybe people at the point of death need to let go of all contacts. Justified or not, I ended up holding onto her wrist.

Now and again, I'd catch her pulse, a quick burst, then it would disappear. At one point, it suddenly got robust, bong, bong, bong—a surprise. It took me a moment to realize that I was picking up my own pulse—which seemed, even at the time, funny. Hospice angel as a total klutz. It was also an ironic reminder that *my* pulse was just fine, thank you very much. Had the weak pulses I'd felt been mine or hers? The blurry boundaries seemed fitting, part of being out of normal time.

Her eyes were closed. Her restlessness passed and her frown smoothed out. She had a little balloon of skin in the bony vee in her throat and it would pulse with each breath. I could see it, even though I could no longer hear her breath. I held onto her wrist and watched her throat. The ballooning became slighter, weaker, with long intervals in between. The process was so subtle that there was no discernable line between her being alive and her being dead, no one obvious moment of passage. Gradually, however, it became clear she was gone. I lifted her head slightly, no response. I kissed her forehead.

"Thank you," I said out loud.

It was about 3:30 A.M. I called the nurse. She came with her stethoscope and listened. Nothing. She wheeled in a machine and attached a blood pressure cuff to Lucy's arm. Nothing. She left.

I rolled down the bed, picked out a clean nightgown for her, and called Frances. A pair of aides came in and quietly and respectfully washed her body. When they turned her over I saw her eyes open wide and her mouth fall open, giving her a look of blank amazement. Had her death come, as she had speculated, as "a shock"? Certainly there had been no outward sign of it.

The next time I looked, her eyes and mouth were closed. The aides had put a pillow under her head. They pulled a clean sheet up to her neck, placed her folded glasses neatly on her chest, and left.

Frances and I hung up. I felt at loose ends. Clearly Lucy was no longer in the body in the bed, but I was finding it hard to leave. I gathered up my tapes and my tape recorder, put them in my sewing bag, rinsed out my thermos of tea. I went out into the hall, then decided to go back into the room and say a formal good-bye. Standing beside the bed, I said a final Hail Mary.

It didn't seem to do the trick. I recited the Our Father, adding on the Protestant coda for her: *"For Thine is the Power and the Glory forever and ever, AMEN."*

But that didn't help either. Then, about a foot over the top of my head, I heard Lucy's voice. "Christine," she scolded, "you go right on home now, you've done everything a body could possibly do." Whatever the source of the voice, it was so *Lucy* that I almost laughed out loud.

My book is back for another round of revisions. I feel at a loss—both with it and with Amber. This morning I call to let her know I'm coming and she's whiny and reluctant: "It's not really necessary. The boys are with their sitter. I'm feeling kind of tired. I've got my soaps to watch."

I tell her we were about to leave on vacation and that since I won't be there next week, I'd like to come on out and see her, if she was up to it.

"I hate to have you drive all that way for nothing."

I go anyway. Same old story: "Wayne resents taking care of me. He wants me to be his mother."

Over the weekend he was sick in bed and she ended up "babysitting the three of them." The laundry (that he was supposed to do) was undone. The cellar steps are too steep for her: she's afraid of falling. "Just looking at them makes me dizzy," she says.

She lets me do a couple loads of wash for her. It's the first time I'd been down in the basement and it smells, not unpleasantly, of earth and machine oil. A weak bulb hanging from a rafter casts a dim light on a waist-high clutter of junk: bed frames, scrap lumber, tools, drifts of dirty clothes, an economy-size box of detergent on an overturned bucket. The place looks chaotic but I have the feeling Wayne knows exactly where everything is. I want to have all the laundry done by the time I leave, but something's wrong with their dryer. After two cycles, the jeans and towels are still wet. She blames it on a failed element. "We don't have enough money to replace it," she says dully.

JULY 2, THURSDAY

Back from Montana feeling restored. It was cold and wet at the ranch. Since it was early in the season, we were practically the only guests and we ended up riding with the wranglers looking for lost horses up in the hills, which, despite the mud and the way the horse slid in it, was really neat. When it rained, we stoked up the woodstove in our cabin and read and drank Bourbon. At the end of the week, the weather cleared and we drove up along the Rocky Mountain Front to the Blackfeet Reservation where my friend Woody Kipp was participating in a Sun Dance. We visited the ceremony briefly, four or five hours only, aware of being white tourists, but joined in the chanting nonetheless. I prayed for Woody and I also prayed for Amber. When I went to visit her this afternoon, I had the idea that she would ask me about my trip to Montana and I would tell her about praying for her out on that high, windy plain and a door would open for us. So much for my agenda!

Her hair is growing in small black tufts. She says it never used to be that dark. On the back of her head, centered above the base of her skull, there's a curious round patch, about the size of a quarter. A large black velvet dot. An effect of radiation?

She kept her appointment with Dr. Houck. She said he thought the radiation must have worked to some degree on her brain tumors or "I'd be drooling by this time." She seems realistic: her hope is not for a cure, but for more time. She is reassured by Houck's assessment that she has stabilized. But in the next breath, she says she can feel the cancer growing in her liver.

She tells me that she discovered the cancer when she went to work at Kmart six years ago. The company's health plan required a physical and when she went for her checkup, the doctor discovered a lump in her breast. She was thirty-two at the time and couldn't believe it was cancer. Her mother's cancer had come later, in her forties and was cervical. So Amber ignored her lump. A year later she found blood in her bra: a discharge from one of her nipples. She went to a different doctor who told her she needed a mastectomy. She ran out of his office. Finally found a third doctor who suggested a lumpectomy and chemo. "I could go for that," she says. He referred her to Houck.

"Wayne blames me for my disease," she says.

Yes, well.

She asks, "Last time you were here, did you change the setting on the dryer?"

I try to remember. "I don't think so."

"Because Wayne woke up in the middle of the night and heard it going. He doesn't want you doing any more laundry."

"You mean it was going all that time? It didn't cut off?"

"I don't know what's wrong with it."

I stare at her. "You could have had a fire. I could have burned you all up!" I apologize profusely.

Three days a week, the boys' sitter takes them to her house, or the town pool, or the library. "They love it," Amber says. Wayne, however, complains about the expense; he still thinks Amber should be taking care of them.

She spends most of the visit unloading about him. She disapproves of the way he manages the family finances. She objects to the large payments he's been making on their debt—a strategy that, I have to say, seems pretty sound to me.

I sit and fold laundry and listen. Finally I ask her the same question I asked Edna: "If you knew you were going to get all better, would you stay with him?"

"No way. I'd trade him in."

It's hard to tell how serious she is. "Would you?"

Her shoulders slump. "No, probably not. He's always been this way." A small mewl of resignation.

Then she hops off the bed and pulls out a greeting card from the top drawer in Wayne's dresser. "I gave it to him for Father's Day," she says proudly as she hands it to me. The card has a cute, kid-like cartoon on the outside, but its printed message is sock-drawer adult: something to the effect that even if we don't have sex, I still love you.

"Oh Amber, that's really nice," I tell her. I'm touched, but also a little embarrassed.

Mare Rockwood still has not been out to see the kids.

When we go into their room to put away clean laundry, Amber discovers that Brett has wet his bed. He's the older one, quiet and painfully shy. Over his bed, a child's artwork is tacked up on the wall along with posters of sci-fi robots. It's a picture of a fish. "Did he do that?" I ask.

"Yeah," she says, preoccupied with the wet sheets.

He has painted an angelfish, striped it with all the colors of the rainbow, and dusted it with gold glitter. It shimmers with hope. "It's beautiful!" I exclaim.

"He's artistic," she concedes.

———

I wash his bedding and (now that the dryer's off-limits) hang it out to dry over railings of the deck off her bedroom. I ask her if hanging out the sheets will embarrass him. She thinks not. "It'll let him know that I know," she says.

She hesitates to tell Wayne. She worries that he'll scold Brett. "What you doin' wettin' your bed, boy?" she mimics. She says Brett used to wet his bed regularly when he was younger but she thought he was over it. She's hoping this is a one-time relapse.

JULY 7, TUESDAY

Finally reach Mare on the phone. I tell her about Brett's bed. She makes a sympathetic noise. She says that she'll try to schedule a visit in a week or two, but right now her calendar is full. Perhaps she has other more responsive patients. First Claire pulling back, then Mare.

I feel I'm on the edge of loving Amber—though I'm not sure what it would take to push me over. Suppose we finally manage to connect. Then what? She dies. I have to wonder if it's worth the effort.

JULY 21, TUESDAY

Back from visiting Andy's mother, Agnes, in Florida. It's the first summer in her life she has not been able to go to her house in northern Michigan; wheelchair-bound and confused, she's stuck in her posh "facility." She puts on a brave face, but is awash in sorrow and anger.

This morning I call Amber and her friend Debby (whom I

have yet to meet) answers the phone. She tells me Amber's tired and is resting. A guarded note in her voice tells me that she is using the phone on Amber's bed: I know that Amber is two feet away, wide-awake and listening.

I feel a thump of disappointment: *She doesn't want to talk to me.*

"She's having a little problem with her voice," Debby went on in a falsely cheerful voice. "She's going to see the doctor tomorrow."

"The doctor over in Winchester?" I ask. "The same one she's been seeing?" Not wanting, for some reason, to say "oncologist."

"Yes."

So maybe it's started. I sent her a postcard from Florida. It took me a long time to pick it out. We were picking out a bunch for Agnes to send to her friends in Michigan: beautiful photos of roseate spoonbills, herons on the wing, plumed egrets, ibises with curving, coral-colored bills. She paid them scant attention: she has let go of her love of birds; she no longer knows their names. Andy helped her with the message, then with a trembling hand she copied it out on each card. "You can't imagine how I miss not being with you," she wrote on the verge of tears.

For Amber, perversely, I picked out an alligator, gleaming darkly in a black swamp, mouth open ready to snap. Like the birds, a oversize postcard with a generous amount of white space on the back. I dropped down an inch and wrote in ballpoint:

Dear Amber,

These critters eat poodles down here. It's so hot and humid that Virginia seems cool!

I sat for about five minutes trying to think of something else to say, and couldn't. I signed it.

Best, Christine

Andy read it. "A little thin."
"Yeah," I agreed glumly.
She probably hasn't gotten it yet. Maybe I should have put "Love."

JULY 27, MONDAY

Back from *my* mother's in Connecticut. Message from Claire on the machine warning me about Amber's "changes." Liver very enlarged, she says.

I go out there and for the first time, I find the house in disarray: breakfast cereal stuck to the dining-room table, the boys' pj's on the living-room floor, Amber in bed and a tangle of clean laundry strewn over the covers. She had started folding then gave up. She looks more bloated in the belly, but I had expected that. What I hadn't expected was her yellow tinge. It is actually fairly becoming, as if she has gotten a tan. And more hair has grown in: soft, jet black commas of it.

Her voice is tiny. "I wish I had it back," she pipes. "I sound like a little old man."

She does. I strain to hear her over the TV. She says the doctor thought she might have tumors on her vocal chords. He told her that her liver was very enlarged. She pulls up her shirt and shows me her rib cage. "It's supposed to be in here but it's all the way down to here." She presses her fingers against her pubic bone.

"Must feel like being pregnant," I sympathize.

"Worse," she squeaks.

Next commercial, she zaps it with the mute and rasps: "I've decided not to worry about money anymore."

I feel a prickle of attention: *What is she telling me?* "That's good," I encourage. But she doesn't elaborate and I don't press. Instead I fold the laundry, two baskets full. I refill her plastic water bottle, pick her lunch-time bowl of noodles off the shag throw rug beside her bed and carry it into the kitchen. I wash the dirty dishes in the sink, wipe the counters, pick up the pajamas off the floor. I use the toilet, flush it, and the damn thing breaks. I lift off the top of the tank and look inside. A strategic piece of plastic has broken. I jerry-rig the innards so that the water stops running and leave a note for Wayne. I seem to have a problem with their machines. First the dryer, now the toilet. That bumbling idiot, he must think.

JULY 30, THURSDAY

After the visit on Monday, I report to Claire's message machine; yesterday she calls back. She seems to be moving into her managerial mode. I sense in her the same relief I've seen in my friend nurse-midwife Anne Holliday when, after a long, tedious labor, the mother finally "gets down to business." Hand-holding gives way to a kind of crisp, medical bustle. Claire has ordered oxygen for Amber and has asked Mare to help her fill out the insurance papers for it. Claire also told Amber that her time of feeling better was a gift, and that now was the time to give whatever she wanted to give to her children, because later on she might not feel up to it.

"What did she say to that?" I wonder.

"She was unresponsive."

Par for the course. I tell Claire that she probably won't deal with the kids. About to go out there now.

Amber is fighting sleep the whole time I'm there. I bring the usual McDonald's meal—she ate maybe three bites of the cheeseburger, one fry. She's rejected Claire's oxygen. "Too expensive," she says. This strikes me as rather brave.

We watch the soaps, I work the background on my needlepoint—mindless stitches in black wool.

Many of the characters on the soaps are now familiar to me, though I still understand very little of what's going on. During the month I was gone, cruelly separated lovers have been reunited, a drug-addict brother has appeared (was he there all along?), a little girl has gone blind in a car crash engineered (accidentally it seems) by her mother (insanely jealous of her ex-husband's girlfriend). The plots tie themselves into knots, but the same smooth faces endure, suffer beautifully in the same studio lighting. They are as untouched as gods and goddesses. They don't *change*. Their story never ends. They are eternal. Does Amber take comfort from this?

Or is it that these faces are her most reliable friends? I keep thinking about how isolated she seems. For better or worse, all my other patients were plugged into a web of family, friends, neighbors: if I did not meet them face-to-face, there was a background hum of their comings and goings. But in Amber's case, except for her constant friend Debby, there is only the empty echo of the meatloaf-bearing missionaries. No one outside of hospice seems to visit. Do people come and she doesn't mention them? What happened to the sister who came at the beginning? I must ask.

I find I don't mind the TV so much anymore—perhaps because I've let go (more of less) of the notion that she ought to be facing her death, preparing her kids, working her way up to Resolution and Acceptance, that high, final plateau mapped out by Elisabeth Kübler-Ross.

But I give it one more try. "Claire's right," I tell her. "Now is a good time to talk to the boys about what is happening to you."

"They know," she squeaks.

"Well," I persist, "think about talking to them about their future, what you wish for them in their lives. It might help them later on, give them something to hold onto."

She says nothing.

I try again. "What do you think it will be like for them without you?"

"It'll be a lot less strict," she says with dry humor.

Then, in the middle of a soap, she tells me she's had a dream. She dreamed that their dog caught a rabbit and she was trying to get the rabbit out of his mouth.

"What kind of rabbit?"

"Just a wild rabbit."

"Like the baby rabbit you rescued from your cat?"

"This one was grown."

I'm straining to hear her over the TV and the air conditioner in the window, but I gather that the dream was a struggle—a frustrating one. She frowns. "I think I got the rabbit free, but I don't know if it lived."

I talk about the concept of dream animals representing aspects of ourselves.

"I don't set much store by dreams," she says.

"I think of them as signposts," I counter. "Sometimes they can tell you where you are." I tell her about my packing dreams: the frustration of packing a suitcase over and over, and with all the wrong clothes; the mounting sense of catastrophe; the panic that wakes me up. "Whenever I have that dream, it tells me that I'm beating my head against the wall, that I need to look at my life and make an adjustment." I offer this casually, with some humor, as if sharing a Hint from Heloise.

She shudders. "I dreamed about my mother a lot."

I stop sewing. "Recently?" I ask, with the all the eagerness of Freud pouncing on a penis.

"No." Eyes on the TV.

"You told me that you dreamed about your mother the morning she died."

"And a lot afterwards, too." She glances at me. "It was pretty frightening."

"Why?"

"Because she was so alive in them."

So I'm still puzzling that one. There seems to be a pattern in her responses. First she denies any interest or connection, then when I say, "Hey, it's okay here, the water's fine," she dips a toe in, ventures into an area of deeper feeling. Will she wade through her fear and reach out to her boys?

My feeling is, that like my mother-in-law Agnes letting go of her birds, she's already let them go.

JULY 31, FRIDAY

Amber harder to shake loose this time. Am I, like Claire, suddenly "up" at the prospect of her death—galvanized by it? Or is it that finally, in our talk of dreams, I felt a connection with her? Saying good-bye to her was different. I took her hand and searched her eyes—looking for what? I leaned forward and kissed her cheek. For a moment, she could have been a much loved daughter. Her skin was very soft, without any odor.

She said, "Your hands are cold."

I realized my feet were too. "It's the air-conditioning, I think."

"Yeah, I don't like it much either," she confided.

"But it's good to have, on a day like this," I said, retreating into banality.

"Yeah." She breathed a small sigh of resignation.

Writing this conversation down, I have to wonder if I really *want* contact after all. Why did I pull back?

If the currency of intimacy is exchange, I'm holding onto my own coin. As trained. This is supposed to be a "fiduciary" relationship. I'm not supposed to unload on her. When she asked me how my trip to Florida was, I didn't confide how awful it was to see Agnes like that. Amber would probably wish that she could live so long. Nonetheless, I'm withholding and, understandably, she keeps her own coin in her pocket. It's as if we're dancing around each other, each clutching our coins, waiting—to do what? Slap them down on the counter? Press them into an open hand?

Anyway, there was a tenderness that passed between us when I kissed her cheek and, however brief it was, it's stayed with me. I'm obsessed again, in the zone, altered. I keep going over her dream, as if it were mine: the dog, a domestic creature chained to the house; the rabbit, wild and free; the deathly struggle between them—God, this whole thing, my *contact* with her, seems so thick and impenetrable—as hopeless as her bulging liver. The image of our pet rabbit's liver comes to mind: dark and smooth against bits of frozen white fur. Our children had named him Hopper. Some dogs had torn him to pieces and I had scooped the remains up on a rusty shovel. It took me an hour with a pickax to hack away a shallow grave in the frozen ground. Timmy, who was six at the time, watched with interest. He didn't seem sad at all.

James Dickey wrote in his journal: "Poetry occurs when the utmost reality and the utmost strangeness coincide." I'm inside a poem?

AUGUST 6, THURSDAY

Claire called early this morning to tell me that Amber died last night. Not clear on the details. It started over the weekend. Her breathing got bad and her short-term memory went. The on-call nurse drove out there to instruct Wayne on signs of imminent death so that he would know what to expect. Monday, he stayed home from work. He told Claire he realized that he couldn't leave her. He was with her the whole time.

I could kick myself for not calling earlier in the week. When I left last time, I told her: "I'll call you Monday or Tuesday, just to check in, then come visit on Thursday." But I didn't call. Our phone calls were such duds to begin with, and on top of that, her voice was going and it was hard for her to use the phone. If I had called, perhaps I would have been part of it. On the other hand, Wayne had my number. Maybe he didn't want me bumbling around breaking something else in the house. It seems apt, in a way, that Amber's death was so private. Claire said he didn't call the sister (with whom, it turns out, Amber still had contact) until after it was over. She thought he was in control, managing it all well. I wonder if there will be a funeral, a viewing. I sort of doubt it. I keep trying to reach him, but there's no answer at the house.

I have the urge, slight and passing, to turn on the soaps in Amber's memory! If she were still alive, I'd be watching them now.

The minimalism of this whole thing is striking. I wonder if I will see a wild rabbit.

AUGUST 8, SATURDAY

Finally got hold of Wayne. A difficult phone call. He grunted acknowledgments of the nice things I said about Amber and was defensive when I asked questions: "Who was there with you?"

"No one."

"What about Debby? Was she there?"

"No."

"The nurse?"

"No."

"Oh. And how are the kids doing?"

"It's not like they didn't have time to get used to the idea."

Several times he told me, "Life must go on." Which—unfairly—made me wonder if he had a girlfriend in the wings. There's to be no service. "She didn't want anything like that," he said.

The end.

Still have the feeling that I'm wandering through empty rooms: a coldly modern museum with polished, echoing floors and angular white walls. Pieces of Amber's life are exhibited in stark isolation. There's a clever avant-garde installation of a TV running a loop of soundless soaps. Her Italian chocolates sit on a pedestal. The eight-by-ten photo of her in sequins as a jazz dancer is mounted on a bare expanse of wall. And there's no nourishment or distraction in this gallery. There are no rich allegories nor long romantic vistas, no clouds, no sunlit seas, no heroic horses, no velvet or armor or veils wafting over plump white breasts, nothing to yearn for or admire, nothing that speaks to me. The space is silent: all I can hear is my own need. Whatever *that* is.

In the last few weeks, I've fixed on the word Intimacy. Is this need a quirk of my own psychology or part of the human condition? It's not like I'm deprived of intimate connections in my "real" life. Why the pull to intimacy with strangers?

But it's also *being on*. That peculiar high of—what? Being outside of time? Being *connected*? And to what? Another individual? The universe? The movement between them?

Well, I know what Claire would say. She talked to Amber about "being united with her Father" and Amber told her she had no desire to see her father, that he was a deadbeat dad. "I mean your Heavenly Father," Claire said. I have to wonder if Amber was pulling her leg—purposefully misunderstanding.

I find I don't have much desire to survive in an afterlife, to survive as me, as Christine Andreae. The idea of not seeing the world through this lens that is me seems rather restful.

Anyway, I was getting worked up, so I called Mare Rockwood and "vented" a bit. Mare, as I now remember from a conversation at the outset, holds that we can all influence each other for the good, even if it's not apparent to us.

"So," I said, "maybe my problem is a lack of faith."

Well, she didn't like that. But really, it would be a relief to have a name for it.

This morning I made bread listening to Albinoni oboes and felt better. Realized in the middle of kneading that I make bread when people die. Even as far back as when my sister Mercy was lost: I remember my sister Jessie weeping on my loaves. I seem to have a kind of instinctive bodily intelligence that doesn't bother about inventing rituals of closure—it just goes ahead and does its thing. So maybe that's the really deep ritual, making food, nourishing ourselves in the face of loss. Funeral services are more surface satisfactions—at least for me. I get to see the family. (And be thanked!) I get some answers. I do feel cheated that I don't get to see what Amber's sister looked like, that I don't get to hear what she had to say about Amber. I wanted to compare notes with Amber's faithful friend Debby. I wanted a look at the kids, to see how they were, how Wayne behaved. Wakes, funerals, burials are *public*. It seems typical of Amber that she (or Wayne) closed the door on her death. It's as if she's saying, *"Deal with your own issues if you want, but butt out of mine."*

AUGUST 13, THURSDAY

No rabbit.

Nice meeting with Mare after an in-service on "customer service." The program was presented by a sweet fellow who manages a mall. The nurses gave him a hard time. He passed out giant chocolate bars—to keep us happy customers, presumably. It worked. I asked Mare if she'd ever had a patient as flatline as Amber. She said no, that she'd always found a spark, even if the person was old, tired, withdrawing, close to death. She saw Amber as intensely private, controlling, grasping, improverished of spirit.

She talked about the necessity of setting self-protective boundaries. "I can't do more for her than she would do for herself, Christine," she said. "I can't care more than she cares."

I had tried to draw my own lines. I had tried to "unpin" myself from Amber each time I left the house. Why did I not see at the time that both Mare and Claire were doing the same thing?

Mare reiterated that she believed I brought some kind of energy into the house that "made a difference."

I'm not so sure. And I'm not sure that "making a difference" matters to me so much. It's the connection, I think—the flow between boundaries that matters—and also that shift into time-lessness that sometimes happens. It never happened with Amber.

Last night I dreamed I was in a play and hadn't learned my

lines. The cast was very supportive and kind, prompting me during the performance. My first entrance had no lines. I went out
on the stage and walked around hunched over a furled black
umbrella, staring at the floor. I muffed my second entrance (of
course) and was saved by a white-faced mime in a clown suit. He
showed me my lines on a script the size of a door. He pointed to a
picture set in the text. It was a black-and-white photo of a little
girl in an Alice-in-Wonderland pinafore. The girl's legs were
limp and splayed like a china doll sitting on a shelf.

The girl-doll was my cue. My line was, "Why?"

I thought: *Well, I can manage that one.* Even in the dream, it
seemed pretty funny.

AUGUST 16, SUNDAY

If, as in hospice-speak, each case is a "journey," perhaps the problem with Amber is that we didn't *move* anywhere.

We were a pair of couch potatoes watching the soaps.

Still haven't written Wayne.

AUGUST 21, FRIDAY

Having agreed to take on a new patient, I finally sat down and
wrote to Wayne. Maybe sometimes you have to move on, step
forward, before you can close the door behind you. It wasn't until
after I called the new patient's house that I was able to write
something about Amber that might be useful later on to the boys.
(If Wayne keeps the letter for them.)

I got the assignment on Tuesday, the eighteenth. A seventy-
six-year-old woman out in Shenandoah Farms. As the roads there
are even worse than Amber's, and as I had the sense of not hav-

ing finished with Amber herself, I put off calling. I tried yesterday and there was no answer. This morning I reached the caregiver, the woman's daughter-in-law. She was a schoolteacher with a soft, pretty voice. She told me that last week she had been desperate for relief, but now her mother-in-law was actively dying and the rest of the family had gathered. The mother was bedridden, unable to eat, and confused. "I have a pot of soup on the back stove for you," she kept telling her son.

So we talked about symbolic messages. About how freeing, how luxurious it felt to have a pot of soup on the stove for one's children. There is no more work to do. She had made supper and it was there for her son, warm and nourishing, whenever he wanted it. "What a wonderful message!" I exclaimed. I was very moved. The schoolteacher was teary and happy. This is what it can be like, I thought. This is what hospice is about: a pot of soup on the stove.

AUGUST 24, MONDAY.

Patient died on the twenty-second. The day after I called. I'm still savoring her pot of soup!

LITTLE FEASTS

In 1881 Pierre-Auguste Renoir spent the winter in his studio working on the large, summery canvas called *The Luncheon of the Boating Party*—the painting that Lucy Wood declared "everyone's favorite." At the time, Renoir was forty years old, a bachelor, and newly in love with his model, the twenty-year old Aline Charigot who was soon to become his wife. The painting depicts a group of friends who have come off the river (in the shimmering background, there are sailboats tacking on the Seine) for a luncheon on the awning-shaded terrace of a garden restaurant. Their meal over, the party lingers around the tables, mingling with the other patrons and finishing up the wine. One of the boaters leans back against the railing. Another straddles his chair, cigarette in hand. Aline, flushed and pretty in a straw bonnet, is cooing at her little dog. It is a sensuous, happy picture filled with light and color. Renoir referred to it as a "little feast." The canvas, however, isn't little; it's almost life-size. It takes up an entire wall of the Phillips Gallery in Washington, D.C., and when you stand in front of it (never alone—it must be the most popular picture in the Phillips' collection), there is the sense that you could easily step right into the moment of that summer afternoon.

Renoir never painted a dark picture. When critics complained that his work was too "pretty," he retorted, "There are sufficient bothersome things in life so that we need not create others." But *The Luncheon of the Boating Party* goes deeper than "pretty." Perhaps the blush of love gave his brush strokes a special radiance. At the same time, he felt the "bothersome" fact of his own mortality breathing down his neck. "I'm not getting any younger," he wrote his friend Paul Berard. "Later I won't be up to the effort; it's hard enough already. . . . It is a good thing from time to time to attempt something beyond one's powers." So perhaps an off-canvas awareness of potential failure and loss served, in some way, to intensify the painting's transcendent glow of satisfaction, its lazy sense of *fullness*.

The Luncheon of the Boating Party seems a perfect picture to hold up as an ending, as the *envoi* to these journeys in hospice. Not simply because it is a celebration of life (to use the funereal cliché). Nor even because it evokes, at least for me, the "zone," that elusive, altered state in which the ordinary becomes luminous and timeless. Renoir's *The Luncheon of the Boating Party*, strikes me as particularly relevant to the end of life because it centers around food.

On the canvas, the forms of the boaters are anchored by a still life (*nature morte*) of their table, up front and center. The white linen tablecloth is rumpled and strewn with crumbs. A stem of grapes lies half-hidden by a discarded napkin. The glasses and wine bottles don't simply catch the afternoon light. Like sacred vessels, they appear to emit their own light. It may be a reach to call the oblong of the table an "altar"—after all, this was hardly a sacrificial feast. But it was a "communion": a group of friends united in the pleasures of good food.

Food is life. And at the end of life, eating is a key issue, if not *the* key issue. When someone we love is sick, our basic impulse is to nourish them. We aim at "building their strength." Our hopes soar when the patient manages to get down three spoonfuls of homemade broth or half a can of Ensure. We let go of green vegetables but can't help feeling dismayed that the patient eats nothing but candy bars. We rejoice when we offer a favorite food, wild strawberries say, and he politely tries one.

"Don't you want some more?" we ask eagerly.

"I don't think so."

We watch the little bowl of berries, picked on hands and knees along the edge of a field. They remain untouched. Inwardly we cry out in despair: *But he loves wild strawberries.*

One of my patients, an older woman with large, guileless blue eyes and four daughters, had a fondness for cheese grits. In the course of her dying, her husband, who had never before set foot in the kitchen, learned how to make the recipe, which his wife— I will call her Katherine—had inherited from her mother. Although he cheated, using instant grits instead of cooking them in a double boiler for an hour as specified in the family recipe, he was as proud of his results as I was of the custards I made for Hal. The weaker Katherine grew, the more grits her husband spooned down her throat. There was a desperation in his feeding that went beyond a fear of losing her. These were guilty grits, seasoned with remorse for his sins against her. These past offenses hung over the family like a thundercloud. The daughters would refer darkly and obliquely to "the way Dad is—you know . . ." and I would nod sagely. But I did not know. If I was vaguely curious, I also had the sneaking feeling that knowing the father's sins was going to make it hard for me to be supportive to him. So I never asked.

Although it was painful for Katherine to swallow, she did not refuse her husband's cheese grits. (Some poetic soul called forgiveness "the scent of violets crushed under one's heel" but in Katherine's case, forgiveness seemed to be the act of swallowing corn mush.) From time to time, the daughters came to relieve their father at her bedside and Katherine had a respite. Her daughters would offer the grits, she would shake her head "no," and the casserole would remain in the fridge. Later, when he learned that his daughters had not, as instructed, given their mother her dose of grits, he would blow up at them. The stuff of comedy. The stuff of tragedy.

I should add that this drama was played out in the family dining room. Since the bedrooms in the house were upstairs, for the sake of convenience, the dining-room table had been removed to make way for a hospital bed. In the same room that Katherine had once fed her family, her family now struggled to feed her. This adaptive use of space is common enough (Lucy Wood's bed had also been installed in her dining room) but for me, it adds a poignancy, if not a dimension of psychic weirdness, to the push and pull over food.

Inevitably, there comes a time—a slow, uncertain stretch of time—when the person who is dying stops eating and drinking. The nurses try to reassure the family. They explain that the patient's body is beginning to shut down; that forcing food and water is unkind and useless. They explain that, contrary to popular opinion, dehydration is a natural and painless course of events: that it lessens swelling, lessens vomiting, lessens the need to urinate, lessens the degree of congestion in the lungs.

Nonetheless, accepting the withholding of food and water as a *comfort* is an exquisitely painful moment for the family. It is a crucial turning point, perhaps more difficult and conflicted than the actual moment of death. To let go of feeding someone we love is a terrible last gift.

When Katherine finally and determinedly closed her mouth to her husband's spoonful of grits, her daughters were relieved. Her husband, however, was distraught. "If she doesn't eat, she'll die!" he exploded.

I met his eyes. I nodded. "Yes," I agreed.

His eyes widened. For maybe two seconds, three at the outside, he got it. He realized that his wife was actually, really and
truly, going to die. Then panic set in. "As soon as she feels better,
I'm going to take her to the beach," he blustered. "She loves the
beach."

There is a large, dark gap between understanding the facts of
death and believing in them. To cross this gap, we must abandon
our "little feasts"—be they as complicated as cheese grits or as
simple as a sip of well water.

As I look back on these pages and the time I spent with Amber, I
have to wonder if I, too, was doing the food thing with her. Not
physically. I had little, if any, emotional investment in the
McDonald's milk shakes I brought her. What I wanted to do was
to feed her *soul*. I brought her poems, prodded at her dreams,
chanted for her out on the empty plains of the Rocky Mountain
Front. Was I trying to push spiritual grits down her throat? Perhaps to fit through death's door, our spirits must close up as well
as our bodies.

It is traditional for the clergy to minister to the dying, but I
think it's probably hard to digest spiritual nourishment on a
deathbed. The physical labor of death is too demanding. In the
fifteen or so cases I've been assigned to as a volunteer, all of my
patients, even the most devout, were more concerned with the
state of their bodies than the state of their souls. Which makes
me think that spiritual food is better taken when we still have a
shot at life. (I am not discounting here the miracle of saving
grace, the last-minute sweep into total connection. But grace is,
by its nature, unpredictable. If grace doesn't descend, a little prior
carbohydrate loading of the soul might be useful.) In any case,
now Amber has joined my ever-expanding circle of ghosts, and
having "written her down," I feel an affection for her. I'm also

beginning to decipher her gifts. One was her emptiness, which (whether a result of her brain tumors or the cumulative effect of habit) has done the invaluable service of showing me my own need—my own emptinesses.

People who read my story of Bivie's death often protest: "How could she *bear* it?" They literally cannot imagine what it would be like to face death with young children in hand. In some cases, the reader feels a bit cheated: as if Bivie did not agonize enough—or I left that part out. But I left nothing out. The fact is, Bivie never talked to me (or broke down and cried) about how hard it was to leave Sara and Olivia. Her maternal pain was an unspoken given in our relationship.

I suspect that by the time I arrived on the scene, Bivie had already done a large part of the work of grieving. Since her diagnosis, almost three months before I met her, she had been facing the prospect of her death. If there were times when she was buoyed by hope or protected by denial, there also must have been times when she imagined what it would be like to die, when she imagined what her children would go through and how they would manage without her. Perhaps, as the physical imperatives of her disease took over and her death became more real, the practical work of arranging day care for Olivia, of teaching Greg to cook chili from her recipe, of cleaning out her closets, offered a kind of relief. Perhaps the imagining of one's death is more charged than the actuality of being *in* the process. I hope this is true.

I don't want to minimize Bivie's suffering—or Amber's—or any other patient's. So I offer the following theory with some trepidation: perhaps, as we close the door on our lives, all things are equal. Saying good-bye to one's cat may be as painful as saying good-bye to a beloved spouse. Not being able to take a shower by oneself may cause as much pain as leaving young children. One of death's older names is The Great Leveler.

At the end of October Andy moved his architectural office into a new building and we spent an afternoon freshening up his drafting tables with new paint. We went out for supper at McDonald's and as we were carrying our trays to a table, I walked past a big man in a clean workshirt. He looked at me oddly and I wondered if I had paint on my face. He took a table and sat down, his square back firmly toward us. It wasn't until I had started eating that I realized it was Wayne. He was sitting with an older man who had gray stubble on his chin. They were drinking coffee and chatting companionably. The body language of Wayne's back was loud and clear: don't talk to me.

Then I noticed that there was a birthday party over in the corner. I thought I spotted Brett. Or was I wrong? There were colored balloons. The mothers were cleaning up half-eaten pieces of cake and torn wrapping paper. They were young and attractive in jeans and pastel tops. The kids were full of energy but well-behaved. I told Andy.

"Which one?" he asked, turning around.

"*Don't stare,*" I murmured.

Then the boy whom I thought was Brett sat down at Wayne's table. A moment later, another boy joined them. There could be no mistake. They were Brett and J J.

The party was winding down. The boys poured out tubes of black and orange candy BBs onto the table and started eating them. Their summer haircuts had grown out. I couldn't take my eyes off them. Were they wearing any of the clothes I'd folded? They looked more alike than I remembered. And bigger and sturdier. Had they grown in the months since I'd last seen them? Or had my memory repackaged them as "poor little motherless sons"?

They had the slightly glazed look of kids who have had too much party, but they sat quietly, trading and eating their Halloween BBs. I had the sense that they were content to be sitting with their father. Although he barely gave them a glance and continued chatting with the older man, Wayne's wide back seemed to make the table a safe place for them.

I felt *very* strange. I was outside looking in. The boys never looked my way. I was invisible. I was a ghost. A curtain had been drawn aside for me and I had been allowed a look at what I had left behind. I saw the boys absorbed in their little feast of black and orange candy. Their life was going on. It was an ordinary life. It might play out badly. It might not. But at that moment, the candy, and sitting with their dad (they were in no hurry to leave), was more important than the death of their mother. I was content to watch—detached, passionless.

I had wanted connection with Amber. Now, as we approached the Feast of All Souls, for an indelible moment in our local McDonald's, it seemed as if I had *become* her.